LIVING FULLY, DYING CONSCIOUSLY

The path to spiritual wellbeing

For my grandchildren and for all the brave souls who are incarnating onto the earth at such a critical time.

LIVING FULLY, DYING CONSCIOUSLY

The path to spiritual wellbeing

by

SUE BRAYNE

www.whitecrowbooks.com

Praise for *Living Fully, Dying Consciously*

Living Fully, Dying Consciously takes you on a profound journey through the rigours of the human condition to understand how spiritual wellbeing generates a healthier world for all of us, and that we are indeed, just passing through this physical existence. Many people understand this following a near-death experience, and it's so good to read a book that wakes you up to the importance of engaging with what mortality really means.

~ **Dr Penny Sartori,** author of *The Wisdom of Near-Death Experiences*

In this time of escalating health needs that no system can hope to meet, Sue Brayne re-acquaints us with the complex truth of the human condition and offers us ways not of curing it, but enduring it - with grace, wisdom, courage and compassion. Her book will make you feel like a better and more complete being.'

~ **Paul Wilson,** lead for prevention, mental health and wellbeing for Bristol, North Somerset and South Gloucestershire

Sue Brayne does not pretend that life is easy. Rather she tackles the heart of the human condition by exploring why so many of us are frightened of death and therefore scared of life. This is a very important book which should be read by young and old alike. Sue's wisdom is profound and we all need to be inspired by her message that living consciously creates a much better world.

~ **Peter Fenwick,** Author, *Shining Light on Transcendence: The unconventional journey of a Neuroscientist*

Sue Brayne's clear no-nonsense approach to living and dying is refreshing and important. Here she shares her wider vision of the meaning of having a human life based on many years of careful work and reflection.

~ **Liz Rothschild,** Director of the Kicking the Bucket Festival, Oxford.

Acknowledgements

I want to thank the Universe for insisting I sit down and write – I fought against it for four years. This book is the result of a deep and profound collaboration.

A huge thank you to Jon Beecher, my White Crow publisher, for saying yes to a metaphorical dog-eared manuscript and turning it into this book. And, a heartfelt thank you to Peter and Elizabeth Fenwick not just for introducing me to Jon, but also for all the wonderful things they have invited me to take part in since we met almost twenty years ago.

To my Power of 8 group, Susie, Amy, Sarah, Beryl, Jeanette, Christine and Jill, who have provided constant support and encouragement. To Graham Lever for invaluable guidance on Mahayana Buddhist teachings and early Christian history. To Helen Baker, dynamite marketing whizz, for calm and wise counsel.

Finally, thank you to everyone who agreed to be interviewed. Your insights, honesty and truths add depth and breadth to what living fully and dying consciously really mean, especially during these times of such uncertainty.

Contents

SECTION 3: THE TRANSPERSONAL

We are all visitors to this time, this place
We are just passing through
Our purpose here is to observe,
To learn, to grow, to love
And then we return home
~ Aboriginal proverb

Other books by Sue Brayne:

The D-Word: Talking about Dying

Nearing the End of Life: A Guide for Relatives and Friends of the Dying

Sex, Meaning and the Menopause

Introduction

Welcome to *Living Fully, Dying Consciously: the path to spiritual wellbeing.*

We are going through times of increasing change and challenge, and it seems to me that many of us are being urgently called to break through centuries of entrenched social, political, colonial and religious programming so we can choose a different way of being: a way of being that really cares about how we live and how we die.

It's time we realised that we are not individual entities aimlessly wandering around the planet. We are deeply and organically connected to each other, to our beautiful, vulnerable Mother Earth and to an extraordinary unseen consciousness, which guides us along our path to spiritual wellbeing.

In ancient times, we naturally celebrated our place within the Universe. However, what we term as progress has insidiously eroded away this deep inner knowing and profound relationship. The result is clear to see.

Separation from the source of who we are makes us scared of life and terrified of death. It fractures societies and creates emotional chaos. It makes us construct stories that aren't true. It creates conspiracy theories that feed our fear. It polarises cultures, politics, faiths and societies. It goads us to fight each other, chuck plastic into our oceans and to arrogantly destroy the very thing that sustains life. Our Earth.

Certainly, there is plenty of goodness to be found in humanity and I never want to lose sight of this. Nonetheless, as I discovered during the past three decades that I have been exploring what living and dying mean to me, many of us have become so embroiled and brainwashed by the craziness of our fast-paced modern world that we end up with an inflated sense of self, which refuses to believe it's mortal. In order to remind us of who we *really* are, the Universe often has to grab us metaphorically by the shoulders and shake us until our teeth rattle. That certainly happened to me.

Thirty years ago, on a beautiful clear mid-August afternoon, I was flying back to White Waltham airfield with a close friend (I have changed his name to Jon) in his two-seated Cessna plane when it fell out of the sky. Against the odds, we both survived.

Jon had just received instructions from air traffic control to drop down from 3,000 feet to 1,500 feet due to the flight path of an aeroplane heading for Heathrow. We levelled out. Then the propeller coughed a couple of times and stopped. For a moment I thought Jon was playing a trick on me, but the colour was already draining from his face as he started to jettison fuel and urgently relayed into the mouthpiece of his headset, 'Mayday! Mayday! We are …' My heart was beating so hard, I didn't catch the rest of the coordinates, which he shouted to air traffic control.

My mind flashed back to a few minutes before I had climbed into the plane. A voice in my head had warned, 'Don't do this.' But I ignored it. Instead, I kissed Jon's girlfriend goodbye, whom we had gone to visit. She was suffering from a painful back injury and recuperating at her parents' home in Sussex. I clambered into the cramped cockpit smelling faintly of engine oil and bumped up and down in my seat as Jon taxied over a mown field that served as a runway, at the end of which hung a limp windsock on its pole. Before I knew it, we were airborne, waving down at Jon's girlfriend.

The Cessna hit an air pocket jolting me back to the present. Ahead in the distance, too far in the distance, I saw White Waltham runway. Jon banked the plane on a wind current as he hunted for somewhere to land. I glanced out of the side window at the sight beneath us. It was harvest time, creating a magical patchwork of golden fields marked out by deep green hedges and small areas of woodland stretching for miles in all directions.

I froze in fear as the plane continued to drop and I began to pray. I didn't believe in God, yet that's who I turned to. 'Please God, let my death be quick and painless.' 'Please God, don't turn me into a paraplegic.' 'Please God, help us.' Faces of family and friends shot through my mind. I said rapid goodbyes to them all.

Below us Jon spotted a playing field surrounded by trees and turned the nose of the plane towards it. I clung onto the sides of my seat, willing the plane to stay aloft for long enough to reach it.

'We're going to make it,' I shouted. 'No, we're not,' he shouted back as we headed straight towards a line of tall poplars. 'Get ready. Get you head down,' he yelled. 'We're going to hit the trees.'

The undercarriage caught the upper branches. There was a mighty thud and tearing sound. The plane violently spun round with shards of windscreen glass pelting into my lap as we crashed to the ground. Then momentary stillness. 'Christ, I am still alive.'

'GET OUT!' Jon screamed. 'Get out before the plane blows up.' I grabbed hold of the twisted door handle and threw myself out.

I heard shouting. Two men were running towards us from a building with fire extinguishers. They slowed down when they saw the plane wasn't on fire. That's when we learned that we had crashed into an army playing field and their cricket net was wrapped around the plane's wheels. The two soldiers who were on weekend duty realised the Cessna was in trouble and raced to get emergency equipment.

I sank to the ground beside the wreckage of the plane, amazed that neither Jon nor I were physically hurt. Yet I felt as if I had been emotionally flayed alive. The word 'sham' came into my head. 'My life is a sham.' I didn't want to know that. I needed a drink. And I needed it now!

Back at the barracks I asked the soldiers for brandy, but they could only offer us tea and biscuits while we waited for a taxi.

I have no idea what Jon and I spoke about during the taxi ride. I said goodbye to him and turned the key in the front door lock of my flat in South London and closed the door behind me. I climbed the stairs, walked blindly into my bedroom, lay down on the bed in the foetal position and pulled the duvet over my head. The faces of my two young sons came into my head. Shame and guilt flooded through me. Five years ago, I walked out of my marriage leaving my two young boys with their father. I saw them as often as I could, but, with no help or support, I struggled to work and care for them at the same time. I threw back the covers and went to the fridge, opened the door and grabbed a bottle of wine.

Standing beside the open fridge door I gulped down one glass and then another. I suddenly realised I wanted to die. I wanted to end the chronic anxiety I was feeling of not knowing who I was; of being such a failure as a mother; of feeling bleak and empty inside and pretending I wasn't.

In my working life, I was a partner in a small corporate film and television production company in London's West End, battling against ferocious competition from other, often larger, production companies. It was turning into a nightmare. I knew I had to tell my business partner that I couldn't do it anymore. But I was too afraid of the consequences. I had no idea where to turn, or what to do about it. I wanted to create a home for my boys, but everything I touched seemed to fall apart.

Rage raced through my body. The plane crash could have been the way out. I could have died a dramatic heroine's death.

Why had I lived?

This question ricocheted around my head for days.

I returned to work, but I lost all interest. Yet I still couldn't bring myself to tell my business partner I wanted out. Fortunately, we won a big budget promotional video, which meant I could go out on location rather than sit in the office and make endless sales calls all day. Even so, the relationship between the two of us became increasingly strained. Something had to give.

It did. My business partner walked out, leaving me with company debts of £30,000. I was too shell-shocked to ask her to pay at least half it. Part of these debts were to self employed cameramen, sound recordists and video editors, all of whom had families to support. I felt honour bound to pay them. I sold my company car and made a commitment to myself that I would do everything I could to pay off what the company owed.

A new salesperson came to join me. He punched life into the company, and we got busier, but my heart wasn't in it. To my shame, rather than taking responsibility for what was really happening to me, I criticised everything my new business partner did.

Within months, both of us realised that this wasn't working so we agreed that I would buy my way out of the remaining debt, now standing at £4,000, leaving him to take over the company.

Cleaned out of savings and desperate for money to pay my mortgage and feed my boys when they came to stay, I took a job as a contracts manager for a television production company. I hated it from the start. Within a short space of time, I was making serious mistakes in the contractual agreements that I drafted. I didn't care. I couldn't see the point in wrapping someone up in legalities anyway. But, again, I was too frightened to give up my salary. How would I afford to live? How could I begin to care for the boys? I started to take days off sick, dragging myself out of bed to lie on my battered old sofa in the sitting room in complete despair, willing myself to die.

It was as if the shock of the plane crash had fractured who I was into tiny pieces. I had no core left. No identity that made sense. And, more terrifying, I had no idea how to find those dissipated parts of me to put myself back together again.

Yet, even when the days became as black as could be, I felt the presence of a tiny chink of light deep, deep inside. That chink of light kept me engaged on some level. All the time, I kept asking myself: 'What's the point of all this?' 'What's the point of life?' 'What's the point of me?' It also made me wonder, 'What *is* that chink of light?'

I believe the intensity of this questioning changed my life. On yet another day off sick, with early spring sunshine spilling through the sitting room window, I had an epiphany. A sentence fell into my head, which said, 'You will become a bereavement counsellor.'

I sat bolt upright. I had no idea where this sentence had come from or how to become a bereavement counsellor, but something began to open up inside me. Then another realisation rolled into my consciousness. I was terrified of life, and unless I did something about it, I would take this terror to my death.

The next day I went into work and resigned. This was the turning point, and things began falling into place. Within a week, a friend gave me a spiritual magazine; in it was an article about Stuart Wilde and his Warrior Wisdom training in Taos, New Mexico. At that time, Stuart was a leading international metaphysical teacher and prolific author of New Age books. As I read the article, I became excited and inspired by Stuart's New Age philosophy and his views on spirituality, metaphysics, and self-empowerment. I loved his irreverent tone and his 'get a life' message. That's exactly what I needed to do. I had to get a life.

I sat down immediately and wrote a letter to his organisation to book my place (this was a long time before emails and the Internet). But how to pay for it?

I went into my bedroom and, from the back of a drawer, I pulled out a worn red leather jewellery box with a brass clip. My mother had presented it to me on my wedding day ten years ago. When I left my marriage, I took nothing with me apart from some clothes and my car. I wanted the boys to be financially secure, so I didn't ask for a divorce settlement. But I did keep the contents of the jewellery box.

I opened the box and looked at two diamond rings sitting side by side in their ring holder. One was a beautiful blue Ceylon sapphire with a crystal-clear diamond on each side, owned by my mother's grandmother. The other was a quarter-carat, yellow solitaire that had belonged to my father's mother. I picked up the sapphire and diamond ring and held it up to the light of the window, making it sparkle. That's what I wanted to do. I wanted to sparkle for myself and for my two sons.

I slipped the ring into my pocket and I went into a jewellery shop in the high street. The jeweller screwed in a monocular to his right eye and bent towards the ring, turning it this way and that. He paused and took out his monocular. 'Where did you get this from?' he asked. I explained its heritage. He offered me a sum I couldn't refuse.

I walked out of the shop, guilt ridden for having sold this precious heirloom, but giving thanks to my great-grandmother for her gift. I was going to Taos, New Mexico.

I flew to America just after Christmas. In Taos I was greeted by deep snowdrifts, pure mountain air and clear blue skies. Stuart's Warrior Wisdom's training took place in a beautiful pueblo-styled hotel complex on the outskirts of Taos. The entire complex was impregnated with the earthly, exotic aroma of burnt sage, which made me feel heady and slightly out of my body.

The course consisted of five intense days that addressed our fears of life. Each day started, at four o'clock in the morning, with a meditation in the group room accompanied by the haunting music of Clannad playing softly in the background. This was followed by a day packed with self-empowerment lectures, exercises and tasks designed to take us beyond ourselves.

In my youth I had been a bit of a dare-devil so finding myself blindfolded and throwing myself off a table backwards into the arms of my fellow participants wasn't a big deal. I loved the high rope challenges, too. I launched myself willingly off a tiny platform at the top of an immensely tall cedar tree yelling, 'I'm an Eagle! I'm an Eagle!' The harness and rope broke my fall with a massive jolt, and I was gently lowered to the ground. The facilitators helped me to my feet. 'You see,' said one, giving me a welcome-back-to-the-ground hug, 'fear is only a mind thing.'

On the last evening, our final test of fear was fire-walking. Stuart was a master at firing us up to the point of hysteria. On a beautifully cold, crisp, clear night, surrounded by the dark silhouette of mountains, with snow on the ground and stars twinkling above us, the earthy smell of burning sage filled our senses as we beat drums and chanted wildly to wait our turn to walk the fire.

When my turn came to face those hot coals, I was ready. I drank in the sound of the drums and the power of the chanting that enveloped me. I took a deep breath, pushed away the fear that was seeping through my body, and stepped forward with purpose. If I could walk on fire, I could do ANYTHING. Within seven strides I reached the other side to be scooped up by two helpers with beaming smiles who put me feet first into a barrel of cold water that reached my calves. Afterwards I checked my feet thoroughly. Not a blister to be seen.

When I arrived back in the UK, I felt ready for anything: but what? I had left my job. I had sold an heirloom. I had walked on fire. I was committed to becoming a far better mother to my boys. But I still had no clue of where my life was heading. I had monthly mortgage payments to meet and I was aware that the money from the sale of my great grandmother's ring was running out.

As luck would have it, a friend left a magazine in my flat with an article about the pioneering work of Elisabeth Kubler-Ross. Elisabeth was a Swiss-American psychiatrist who was one of the first doctors to recognise the spiritual and emotional needs of dying patients. She introduced her theory of the five stages of grief in her ground-breaking book *On Death and Dying*, which became a definitive guide for anyone working with the dying, for relatives of the dying, and for the dying themselves.

At the end of the article was information about a week-long training course to become a Life, Death, and Transition facilitator with the Elisabeth Kubler-Ross Foundation. The training was held on Vashon Island just off the coast from Seattle in

Washington State. I felt a rush of excitement. This aligned perfectly with my epiphany of becoming a bereavement counsellor. Yes, it did mean another trip to America, but I knew I had to go.

Together with a friend, also inspired by Elisabeth Kubler-Ross's work, we flew to the West coast of America and took a boat to Vashon Island without a clue of what lay ahead of us. In our naivety, we thought the training would be week-long lectures in how to support the dying and the bereaved. But we were mystified as to why we had been instructed to bring a torch and a pair of gardening gloves. 'Maybe we will be gardening by night,' my friend joked.

Upon our arrival we were ushered into a cosy log cabin with two-tier bunk beds set against all four walls. Our cabin was one of a number on the complex, built for participants. These cabins nestled amongst red alder and fir trees. The smell of pine cones filled the damp air.

As dusk fell around a hundred of us (my friend and I were the only British people) gathered together in a large room in the main cabin. Nine facilitators welcomed us and spoke about how they had been inspired by Elisabeth Kubler-Ross's work and her profound understanding of grief and loss. Inspiration flooded through me, too. I would return home and fix everyone's grief.

My excitement increased until the lead facilitator asked the group at the end of the evening, 'Who is afraid?' Hands shot up.

'Yes', he said, 'you should be.'

My friend and I glanced at each other. What had we signed up for? We decided it probably wasn't gardening by night. We had already discovered that we needed our torches to light our way along the dark path to our bunks in the evening.

The following morning, we gathered together again in the main log cabin. Our nine facilitators were waiting for us, seated on chairs in a row behind a mattress lying on the floor. Thick telephone books were piled up at the side with a solid plastic yellow bat leaning against them. I still had no idea what was going on.

'Who's first?', the lead facilitator said.

A middle-aged woman with dyed blonde hair and a care-worn face clambered onto the mattress. She pulled on her gardening gloves, placed several telephone books in front of her on the mattress, grasped hold of the bat and started beating the books with all her might, screaming with rage that her abusive husband had abandoned her for someone else. The air turned thick with anger and grief as people, touched by her pain, began to weep and sob with her.

I shrank in horror. I was brought up never to express what I was feeling. It wasn't done. No matter what happened you just got on with it. Anything remotely unpleasant was swept under the carpet. I may have walked on fire, but this was NOT what I had signed up for.

I have no idea how I got through the two days as, one after another, participants got onto the mattress to express their rage and grief of what had happened to them. I was so out of my middle-class British comfort zone – it was so unlike any experience I had ever encountered before – that my mind blanked most of the details of those tragic stories. And, I certainly wasn't prepared to confess to a bunch of strangers that I was overwhelmed by the grief and shame of leaving my boys.

I suppose I could have walked out yet something kept me there. Three days in and I was still trying to get used to the screaming and sobbing, but – most of all – to the compassionate holding of the facilitators. I had never come across people who listened with such attention and love. They noticed everything and that frightened me even more. Someone else got onto the mattress and started to sob. I made a bolt for the door and leant against the railing of the wooden balustrade that surrounded the outside of the log cabin taking deep breaths.

'When would you like to come to the mattress?' asked the facilitator who had come to find me. She was in her fifties – tall and slim with long dark hair and a gentle face – a doctor by trade. We stood, side by side, underneath the eaves. The mist and drizzle created the kind of thick grey light that, I imagined, a medieval knight could come riding out of to take me away to some other land where screaming and sobbing never happened.

The facilitator turned to me expectantly. 'I don't really think I need to do that,' I said, stepping back from her. 'I'm fine. My life is fine. I mean, nothing bad has happened to me. I mean ...' I trailed off as she raised an eyebrow. 'Nothing like that.' I flicked my head towards the group room.

'Well, think about it,' said the facilitator. She looked me straight in the eye. 'Elisabeth's work is about owning your pain so you can let go and die at peace. And, you can't help anyone else until you've dealt with your own shit.' I felt shame burn across my cheeks.

Together we returned to the room.

On the last day I did get onto the mattress. I did not put on my gardening gloves and I didn't reach for the telephone books or the bat. I did not admit that I had left my children with their father because I had a mental breakdown of some kind. Instead, I sat on the mattress and told the group how grateful I was to my parents and how I had never experienced any kind of abuse. This is true. Neither of my parents laid a finger on me. However, I had no idea how my childhood conditioning had prevented me from growing into a mature adult.

I flew home feeling confused and disorientated. Still, I felt a calling to continue to train as a Life, Death, and Transition facilitator, as training was being offered in Ireland and the UK. Even so, it took months of witnessing other people's courage to deal with their pain and grief, finally to be brave enough to get onto the mattress and admit I was sitting on a shame and rage so huge I had the capacity to kill. This was truly liberating. And, I also realised that it was my inner wisdom or flash of spiritual wellbeing – that chink of light deep inside – that had kept me going after the plane crash.

Since those tumultuous teeth-rattling days, I have dedicated my life to understanding what it means to live and die, and how spiritual wellbeing is about connecting with the core of who we are and acknowledging the awe of being part of something so much greater. I also believe that spiritual wellbeing will motivate us all to come together to cope with the immense changes that we face. Across the globe, people of all ages, creeds and colour are rising up to express a desire to do things differently.

This gives me such hope and reminds me that I am part of an invisible, potent collective that is breaking down barriers of what no longer serves the world, and turning limitation and fear into a determination to do things better, so that future generations can continue to experience life on Earth.

Looking back, I can see how this something greater has guided me and sometimes hauled me along my path. Scientists refer to it as The Field, the Unified Field, or Quantum Consciousness.[i] Some people call it Universal Intelligence or Universal Consciousness. Some call it, God, or the Light, or the Source, or Great Spirit. Others call it the Great Creator, Brahma, or Great Mystery. Others simply call it love. I spell this Love with a capital L because for me this higher Love is about a transcendent state of grace, acceptance and compassion – completely different from the rigours of human love.

It doesn't matter what we call it. But I believe it does matter that we turn towards this vibrant loving force and allow it to guide us forward.

As I have said already, we lose sight of what's important as we struggle to make sense of our increasingly fractured and frenetic twenty-first century world. Yet, even though we are facing an enormous unknown, when we understand that this physical life is about learning to accept our mortality so we can treasure and nurture the life we have and the planet we live on, we can make peace with who we are no matter what storms are raging around us.

I am the first one to admit that the human journey is far from easy. At times I have found life insanely painful, confusing and lonely. But I don't think it can be easy at this present time in human evolution. To redress the troubles and damage we have brought upon ourselves, and to cope with the planetary changes that we face, the whole of humanity needs to shift to a new level of consciousness. We are quickly learning that the reason for life is not about the label we wear on our lapel or obtaining more possessions: it's about WAKING UP and taking responsibility for everything we create individually and collectively. Our fear of death lessens when we know we have done everything we can to make life a better, more sacred experience. This, for me, is worth dying for.

Before We Start

Before I introduce the structure of the book, I think it's important to explain where my path to spiritual wellbeing has led me. I am not a bereavement counsellor in the traditional sense that my epiphany led me to believe might happen after the plane crash. Rather my calling is to run groups, workshops and retreats, which help people to talk honestly and openly about what it means to live and die in this time of global change (recently I launched Living Consciously for Better World community Facebook page[ii] to support this work).

Apart from the joy of welcoming grandchildren into my life, my path led me to complete two MAs – the first in the Rhetoric and Rituals of Death from Southampton University; the second in Creative Writing at Oxford Brookes – and to train as a psychotherapist specialising in trauma, grief and loss. My journey through the menopause inspired me to write *Sex, Meaning and the Menopause*, and my work as a researcher on a five-year retrospective study into end-of-life experiences further inspired me to write *The D-Word: talking about dying* and the booklet *Nearing the End-of-Life: a guide for family, friends and carers*, which I co-authored with Dr Peter Fenwick who led the end-of-life research study.

To date, I have hosted over thirty Death Cafés, which provide a safe space for people to talk about death and dying without the fear of being told they are morbid or that they may upset someone, or because they want to talk freely about their fear of dying or the death of someone they love.

Death Café[iii] was set up by Jon Underwood in 2011. He was inspired by the work of Bernard Crettaz, a Swiss Psychologist who ran the first Death Café in Switzerland. Jon loved the concept of a chat about death over tea and cake, so he and his mum, Sue Barsky Reid, also a psychotherapist, launched the first Death Café in London.

Since the Death Café website was set up, Death Cafés have spread throughout the world. Jon died in 2017 age 44 of undiagnosed leukemia, leaving behind his wife and two young children. I am so glad I had the privilege of meeting him and making him a cup of tea. I am particularly thrilled to be part of a movement set up by Jon to change and challenge the way we talk about death and dying.

But, most of all, this book draws on 66 grit-in-the-eye years of absorbing what it takes to live fully so, when my times comes, I can do what I can to die fully conscious. Therefore, I sincerely hope this book contributes to your way forward and helps you to appreciate how much your life and death really matter.

What This Book Is About

Living Fully, Dying Consciously does not follow a particular philosophy, religious belief or spiritual discipline. Since I embarked on my path to spiritual wellbeing, I have encountered many teachings, insights, philosophies and research that have spoken to me and helped me to persist with this mad thing called human life.

Over the past few years I have also become increasingly fascinated by scientific research into quantum consciousness. It's exciting to me that systematic scientific study is putting factual substance behind age-old mystical concepts and indigenous beliefs that speak of the Universe as an intelligent force. Science and spirituality are finally meeting. This again gives me hope that we *will* find a way for the world to thrive, even if it's in a manner we cannot imagine right now.

However, I want to be clear that *I don't have answers for anyone else.* Yes, we belong to a greater collective, but life is a truly personal experience. Therefore, my offer is to share what has helped me to wake up and acknowledge the power and strength of my mortality, and how this inspires me to engage with others who want to develop a deeper understanding of spiritual wellbeing and how to use it in service to our changing world. I do not consider this book to be an academic study on any level. However, I have included a number of citations in each chapter in case you want to follow up the references I mention.

Structure Of The Book

I have divided the book into three sections. The first section explores why we are afraid of living. The second section delves into how our psychological blocks prevent us from dying consciously. The final section focuses on opening up to the transpersonal side of who we are, our dying process and what may happen after we die.

I realise life cannot be separated into nice neat linear sections; if only things could be that simple. However, I have used this structure because of my own experience of developing spiritual wellbeing. I noticed that I went through a process: first, I had to acknowledge I was virtually paralysed by the fear of life; second, I began to understand that I had a lot of inner work to do if I was going make peace with my mortality; third, my psychological healing opened up space inside me to explore the transpersonal side of who I am, and my connection with universal consciousness.

The closing chapter looks at how present global changes appear to be part of a much greater evolutionary shift for all life on Earth and how we can consciously and responsibly engage with what we are all facing. I have included this chapter because, to me, it really matters that we go beyond our limitations and come together to support each other as we sail into the unknown.

Each chapter concludes with a health professional who speaks about what living fully and dying consciously means to them. I have also included shorter personal interviews throughout the book. Names have been changed to protect identities.

You can either read this book as a progressive personal journey or dip in and out of sections which draw your attention. All I invite you to do is to hold the awareness that every human being on the planet is also trying to make sense of life and death.

SECTION 1:

THE FEAR OF LIVING
FULLY

CHAPTER 1

WHY ARE WE SO AFRAID OF DEATH?

The climate crisis is slapping death in our face. Extinction of species (including humans) is now mentioned almost daily on mainstream media. But, how can we begin to confront the enormity of this if we can't accept or talk about our mortality? So, for now I am parking the climate crisis to focus on what engaging with our own death brings up for us. There seems to be a common belief that death is a taboo subject. I disagree. In my experience of talking to many people about death and dying, it's not that they don't want to talk about it – they are usually desperate to have the conversation. The problem is they don't know *how to* talk about it. Quite simply, they have never been taught.

These questions have been posed by participants who come to the Death Cafés.

Will it be painful?
Will I know what's happening?
Is there life after death?
How will my parents survive without me?
Will I simply cease to exist?
Have I wasted my life?
Will I be forgotten?
Will I go into nothingness when I die?
What will happen to my children when I die?
Will God punish me for what I did?
Will 'I' still continue without my body?
How will my spouse cope without me?
What can I do to escape death?
What have I done to leave this world a better place?
Will I go to hell or to heaven?

Ignorance

Anxiety about death is different for all of us, and often depends on our personal, religious and spiritual beliefs. Nevertheless, while talking to interviewees who contributed to *The D-Word: talking about dying*, I realised that most of us in Western cultures fear death because we are ignorant about it. Perhaps this is a strange comment given how exposed we are to it twenty-four hours a day.

The news media continually floods our awareness with tragic and horrific images and stories of war, murder, violence, terrorist attacks, famine, refugee crises, natural disasters and, more recently, the rampant extinction of species, all of which remind us that death is an ever-present reality. However, being bombarded with images and reports of human suffering is causing desensitisation. It is just too overwhelming to take on board, so we push the thought of death away.

Paul Slovic, a psychologist from the University of Oregon[1], says there's a radical loss in sensitivity towards large groups of suffering people. We are far more moved to act when we empathise with an individual's story. He uses the example of the Syrian war when thousands of people had died, but the West only really woke up to this when a photograph was published of Aylan, a three-year-old Syrian boy of Kurdish descent, whose little body was washed up on the beach in Turkey on 4, September 2015. This galvanised people to raise money for Syrian refugees. But this, he says, only lasted for about a month. More recently the images of the bodies of migrant Oscar Matinez and his young daughter, who both drowned during an attempt to cross the Rio Grande from Mexico into the US, caused international outrage. But, again, this outrage receded as more tragic stories about the global plight of migrants, desperate to make a better life for themselves, are brought to our attention. We may want to help, but it becomes a case of 'not in my back-yard.'

Death happens to others, not to us

Films, TV dramas and novels also distort our relationship with death by presenting us with the perfect end, which is usually shown by someone taking a final sigh and closing their eyes as their loving family (one of whom has just arrived in the nick of time for a tear-jerking reconciliation) softly weep around the deathbed. Or death is portrayed through thrillers, gangster movies, and horror films as brutal, violent or macabre.

In reality, of the 55.3 million of us who die each year across the world[2], most of us will die of natural causes brought about by old age even though doctors rarely register this as the cause of death. It appears that we are not allowed to die of old age. A disease or illness is usually stated instead.

Yet, relatively few of us, particularly in our modernised Western cultures, have much idea of what death looks like, what it smells like, what it sounds like, or indeed, what the actual dying process entails. We have little idea of the impact that the death has on family relationships either.

I have many people coming to my Death Cafés, workshops and retreats who still have elderly parents alive even though they, themselves, are in their sixties and even early seventies. One participant in his seventies described the fact he had never been exposed to a death of someone close as 'shaming.' Many participants say that although they may have sat beside someone who is dying, they were not present at the time of death. Others say they have never seen a dead body and that makes them frightened of death. This would have been unheard of before the Second World War, where most deaths happened at home.

We've lost the skill of death and dying

We may now be living in hi-tech magic land, but it is clear to me that this has created a culture devoid of skills that enable us to be present and attuned to death and dying. Death may happen to other people but not to us, and the very thought of our mortality fills us with fear and dread. I believe that this fear and dread drives our obsession with the multi-trillion-dollar anti-ageing industry that pervades our lives. The cosmetic surgery industry in the UK alone is worth £3.6 billion[3], and respected health and beauty magazines such as *Harper Bazaar*, aimed at 'discerning ladies', frequently run feel-good articles about women who have face-lifts in their mid-thirties. Not so long ago I heard a Radio 4 discussion on how sixteen-year olds are having Botox injections, which are readily available on the high street. Something has gone very awry here. If we are constantly obsessing about our outward appearance, we disconnect with our inner self, with each other and what's really important.

Of course, it's great to look good but it appears to me that we are being brainwashed into fighting the ageing process, because ageing in our society means decay and death. But, no matter how hard we try to evade ageing and no matter what we do to our bodies, nature's evolutionary process *always* wins. We will age. We will grow old. We will die. It is utterly inevitable.

I see the denial of ageing and death as being responsible for creating narcissistic self-obsessed societies, which, says the Dalai Lama, makes us greedier, angrier, more selfish and more vengeful, and this generates a world of fear, suspicion and animosity. Considering how every generation in our Western society is struggling to cope with fear, loneliness, and isolation I believe he is right. Then take a look at the state of our natural world, our source of life. This acutely mirrors how disconnected we have become from our own mortality.

Death is 'awful'

Furthermore, our twenty-first century youth-addicted culture bombards us with media stories about the importance of preserving and extending life instead of accepting that death is a natural part of the human condition. Rather than thinking of death as a release from the physical world, we speak of death as 'awful,' 'dreadful,' 'sad' and 'a terrible waste' (even if the person is ninety-five). Yes, death can be tragic and hard to bear especially when babies, children, young people and young parents die; but, for many who have a terminal illness, are experiencing great pain, or have reached old age, it is a release. Yet, in my experience of listening to many relatives speak of this sense of relief, they often qualify it by stating something along the lines of, 'I feel so awful for saying this,' or 'I feel so guilty that I should feel relief.' Therefore, the grieving process becomes enmeshed in shame and guilt. This stops us from talking honestly and openly about death, or having difficult conversations with the dying, or knowing what to say to those who are bereaved.

Many participants who come on my workshops, retreats, and Death Cafés talk about their fear of saying the wrong thing or making things worse. 'I don't know how to say what I want to say to my mother,' said one participant. 'She hasn't got much longer to live. And what we haven't said to each other seems to hang in the air between us. It's very uncomfortable.' Another said, 'I don't want to cause an upset in the family by naming what's really going on with my father. I want to talk about it, but I know my sister and my mother don't. It makes me feel really lonely.'

The other side of the coin is people turning away from the bereaved. 'A few months after my daughter died, I felt a need to talk to someone, so I knocked on my neighbour's door,' said a Death Café participant. 'She and I had always been on friendly terms, and of course she knew about the death of my daughter. She opened the door and looked at me in horror. I knew instantly I had made a mistake, so I backed away. Since then she has virtually ignored me. I found that so hurtful. But I also understand that she found it too difficult to talk to me.'

Many other participants have had similar experiences. For example, a number of bereaved people talk of friends literally crossing the street rather than speaking to them. 'It's as if I had a disease and they were terrified they were going to catch it,' said one person. 'You certainly find out who your friends are when someone dies,' said another workshop participant.

We are shielded from death

Participants also talk about being shielded from what's really going by the amount of medical treatments they undergo, or their sick relative has. On average someone who has a terminal illness (whether they know or not) will, in his or her final year of life, visit a hospital over thirty times. Therefore, rather than focusing on pastoral or spiritual care, the dying process centres around various tests the person is having, whether their treatment and medication is working, the number of appointments lined up with medical specialists, and conversations about life threatening conditions turn into medical jargon. 'Your lymphocytes are up (or down).' 'Your x-ray shows a shadow on your superior lobe.' 'Your next appointment is with the oncologist.'

'I spent most of last year in a car heading for the hospital with my husband,' said a workshop participant. 'I was completely exhausted and everything we planned had to be worked around my husband's next appointment. I became quite resentful. I would rather have spent his last year enjoying what time we had left together.'

I find this really sad. I, and everyone who picks up this book, will die sooner or later. None of us know how long we have left. This is one great mystery that we can't conquer, and long may it be so. But, how can we engage in what it means to live fully and die consciously when we refuse to age, find it hard to separate guilt and shame from death, become embroiled in medical treatments and confused by medical jargon? I see this as radically separating us from accepting that death at any age, however tragic, is a part of the human condition.

You are not allowed to die!

The desperation and urgency to hang onto life at any cost has created a society that looks to medical science to fix death, cure it and even stop it. And when it doesn't, we turn to litigation to punish those who have allowed it to happen.

I was profoundly disturbed when I read about a care-home nurse who, in 2015, was found guilty of misconduct when he failed to attempt resuscitation on a frail elderly resident[4]. It seemed that the resident had died five minutes or so before. Instead of calling the emergency resuscitation team, the carer called the non-emergency helpline an hour later. However, since a Do Not Attempt Resuscitation (DNARCPR) order was not in place for the patient, the carer was expected to attempt CPR (cardiopulmonary resuscitation) even though the person had died.

Anyone who has been on a CPR training course knows that you have to exert extreme pressure on the sternum bone to make the heart beat again, even if it does mean breaking the person's ribs. What a terrible thing to inflict on an elderly person approach the end of life. Was this carer really negligent? Or was he being humane?

A friend told me another deeply distressing story about her ninety-six-year-old godmother who had been living for many years in a residential home. She told me,

> My godmother was informed she had to have a new pacemaker. She needed to be admitted into hospital and receive specialist care afterwards. This meant she would not be able to return to her residential home where she had lived for years as they did not provide nursing care. My godmother would have to find somewhere else to go. This was extremely distressing for her and for all of us who loved her. Fortunately, she died shortly before she was to have the new pacemaker fitted.

I have heard many similar stories. To me, the overall message is that death is a tragic failure and to be avoided at all costs. In fact, several billionaires are currently investing vast amounts of their wealth into the hedge fund, Palo Alto Investors, located in California. The hedge fund sponsors the Longevity Prize for anti-aging research[5]. Its goal is to discover immortality and a number of these hedge fund sponsors have set up trust funds for their future 'resurrection.'

This is not new. In 1974, James Bedford was the first person to have his dead body frozen through cryogenics (freezing at very low temperatures). At the end of 2018, Alcor, an American company which offers cryogenic services, reported it has 122 male 'patients' and 42 female 'patients'[6] all of whom have had their bodies frozen in hope that they will be revived when science has progressed enough to bring them back to life.

Other cultures

Eastern Traditions such as Buddhism and Hinduism have a completely different perception of the life and death process, and many native cultures and first nation people, dating back to ancient times, believe that they are part of a miraculous dynamic energy which guides them from cradle to the grave and beyond. They regard life as a karmic circle, a spiral or wheel of existence that continues to evolve over lifetimes and to look at each physical life, while it lasts, as a gift of learning and spiritual awakening. Death is viewed as an onward journey and a preparation time for returning into a physical body in order to progress spiritually life after life until they reach the point of enlightenment.

Oglala Lakota Chief Low Dog who lived during the 1800s is reported to have said, 'This is a good day to die'[7], expressing his openness to death happening in any moment and how he had no regrets or unfinished business. I find this incredibly moving and empowering. It makes me want to throw my arms wide open to expand my understanding of spiritual wellbeing every day for the rest of my life so I can welcome my death when it arrives. I want to feel utterly spent and ready.

This is why I am inspired when I hear of people such as my friend Sarah who consciously chose to take back control of her dying process in a society that finds this deeply uncomfortable.

I want to die my way

I met Sarah over twenty year ago and was terribly sad when she was diagnosed first with Parkinson's disease and then struck down by a severe stroke. She was aged seventy-two at the time.

Sarah had always been a feisty person, fiercely fit and independent. With an enormous rucksack strapped to her back, she led numerous groups on walking tours through her beloved Italian countryside, thrilled to be introducing her charges to local wines and delicious food. She would also disappear on long solo excursions to research and write European walking guides.

Even after she retired, Sarah loved to travel. At the age of sixty-four she gave up her rented cottage in the south of England and set off around the world for three years. I would receive hellos on postcards from far-flung places such Patagonia, Easter Island, Mongolia and Tibet. It made me green with envy. She returned to the UK and bought a small house in Wiltshire, turning her long, narrow over-grown garden into a thriving bird sanctuary.

Just after her Parkinson's diagnosis we were sitting outside on her small patio in the heat of summer when she asked me to be her first point of contact in an emergency. 'I know you will be able to handle it,' she said, looking at me from under the brim of her battered old sun hat. I knew she was asking me to help her fight to die if necessary.

We proceeded to talk about her death, and how she wanted to end her life. She told me she wasn't afraid to die. She didn't particularly believe in reincarnation, but she believed she would be with her mother who had died several years earlier. Sarah missed her mother dreadfully and was convinced she would be reunited with her. We also spoke about her desire to go to Dignitas in Switzerland rather than end her life as a helpless old woman. I told her if she ever wanted to go, I would go with her.

But this was not to be. Not long after, I received a call from an emergency responder. He had broken into her house to find her on her bed unable to move because of a stroke. Somehow, she had managed to make a call to 999 from her mobile which she kept on her bedside table. The emergency responder told me he had found instructions on her desk of what she wanted in case of an emergency and my name had been at the top of her contacts list.

Sarah was taken to hospital by the paramedics and stabilised. I arrived a few hours later. Since she was unable to speak coherently, she urged me through hand signals and slurred speech to communicate to medical staff that she did not want to receive life extending treatment or to be resuscitated. I called to a nurse and with Sarah nodding vigorously from her bed, I communicated her wishes. Much to her relief, these were recorded in her notes.

But death doesn't happen that quickly. As she had been so fit throughout her life, Sarah made progress and began to receive physiotherapy sessions and other treatments. This enabled her to communicate on her tablet using her good hand. After a few weeks she was moved to another hospital for further rehabilitation.

Over the following weeks she lost a huge amount of weight. Her hazel eyes, once so full of mischief, became unnaturally large and dull and her iron grey hair hung in limp strands to her shoulders. But for me the most distressing thing was to see how her cheeks had sunk into her waxy-white face that had for so many years been suntanned, vibrant and healthy.

After three months of rehabilitation she was allowed home with full time live-in care. But she hated her space being invaded by strangers even if they were carers and she hated even more having her dignity stripped away. 'Can't even wipe my own arse,' she wrote on her tablet to me.

When she intimated to her eighty-year old sister that she was probably dying, her sister refused to accept it. Sarah communicated to me that was very difficult for her. 'I want her to know. I want her to talk to me about it but she won't have it.'

I went to see Sarah shortly before she was admitted back into hospital. By this stage she was in considerable pain. I took a seat beside her wheelchair and together we sat on her sun-filled patio watching the small garden birds that she adored fight over the bird feeder. I then walked beside her as her carer pushed her wheelchair up the garden. She indicated to me to take a pot full of raspberry canes and a tree peony, which are now growing in my own garden.

When her carer had gone to make us some tea, she looked at me beseechingly. 'I want to die,' she said taking a breath between each word so I would fathom her slurs. Her words may have been hard to understand but I knew exactly what she was saying to me. 'Help me.'

'I can't, Sarah. It would be murder.'

'I know,' she said. 'But this is shit.'

Shortly afterwards, Sarah asked to be readmitted into hospital. I believe she planned to be readmitted because she was desperate to die. She had had enough of suffering, and she wanted to take control of her death. A family member told me she communicated via her tablet to the nursing staff that she wanted to talk to doctors with members of her family present. During the meeting she wrote down clear instruction on her tablet that she no longer wanted to receive life extending treatment and signed a Treatment Escalation Plan (TEP) and Resuscitation Decision Record declaring she was of sound mind. She then turned her face to the wall. It took a further two weeks before the end came.

I spoke to her sister shortly after she died. Her sister told me, 'Sarah was virtually unconscious and unable to verbally communicate, but the day before she died, she looked me in the eye and slowly raised her thumb as if to give me the thumbs up. I knew she was saying she was so happy to be off.'

I found that very comforting.

I am in awe of Sarah's decision to sign that form even though she knew no-one could help her along her way. She also knew she was in for a rough ride for a while – she was fully aware that it takes time to die – but she wanted to go home to her mother, and that was more important to her than staying alive, incapable of taking care of herself.

Sarah's example teaches us to really think about the way we want to end our life. We all need to consider how to communicate our desires to medical staff, family and friends so they can accompany us on our journey towards death rather than pretend it isn't happening. When we don't communicate with each other, it puts additional stress onto an already fraught situation.

A recent study by Sue Ryder charity reveals that 68% of people who took part have not made a Will, 67% do not know they can choose where they want to die and 70% have not spoken to family or friends about dying. This *really* needs to change

Here are a few practical pointers to encourage you to start talking about the D-word so you don't leave an unnecessary mess behind:

- Writing a Will is part of the process of accepting our mortality.
- Making a Living Will (also known as an Advance Directive) helps us to take control over what kind of end of life care we would like to receive. This may be viewed as a legal document, therefore medical staff will consult it and take note of our wishes if we are not in a fit state to communicate them ourselves.
- Appointing a Power of Attorney while we are mentally able, enables us to pass on responsibility for our financial affairs to someone we trust when we are no longer able deal with them.
- Telling your family that you want to have a conversation about your funeral. How will they know what you want if you don't tell them?
- Clearing out your loft, garage and cupboards! Someone's got to do it.

Mireille Hayden, death doula and co-founder of Gentle Dusk, which provides training and support for end of life planning, dedicates her life to helping people to talk about what really matters.

I love what I do. It's my passion to help people to talk about anything to do with death, dying and grief. Yes, it's hard at times. And, yes it does make me cry at times. But that's okay too. The trouble is that we have created a society where we are terrified of our own pain, other people's pain, or inflicting pain onto anyone else. But this negates any deep emotion we have. We can't discuss anger, sadness or death. It's not done. And, we push this onto our children too. We can't bear the thought of our children feeling pain.

This means that we are creating generations with no-one to talk to about what really matters. But, if we're not able to admit to immense pain, or we're told that it isn't 'right' to talk about it, of course this makes us afraid of death. I think modern medicine has a lot to answer for. It's made us feel invincible. Rather than accepting death, however painful it can be, as a natural part of life we fill our lives with material possessions. In fact, it seems to me that the aim of life has turned into one of accumulation.

This makes us very overly protective of everything we have, including our life and our family. I saw this when I was accompanying a young mother in her forties through her dying process. She had two older children and one still at school. She couldn't bear the thought of what would happen to her younger son. So, she entered into a battle with death by agreeing to any treatment that would keep her alive for a little while longer. Some of the treatment was truly horrendous, but she kept having it right up to the very end. I found this very hard to witness. I felt that it would have been so much better for her family to have had the time to say their goodbyes, discuss what needed to happen for everyone, and find ways to support her children.

However, I have learnt over years of working in this area that you can't do anything with people who won't accept they are dying. On the other hand, when I am running training course, I take great joy in watching people open up to talk about death and dying, maybe for the first time. Something changes in their consciousness and they see something about themselves they may have never connected with before. It is not unusual for someone to say, 'I realise I am in the wrong job. I have got to do what I really want to do.'

I find that deeply satisfying. I want to die in full awareness, and if that means I have physical and psychological pain, so be it. I see pain as transformative. I believe that we take what we create in our physical life into the afterlife as well. So, I want to continue transforming until I take my final breath. This gives my life purpose.

The following chapter provides a brief and *very* broad historical overview suggesting why many of us in the UK have developed such a distorted view of death, why we are reticence to speak openly about death and dying and why Christianity has shunned Eastern concepts on reincarnation or rebirth. I think this is important to include because even through the UK is now a multi-faith society, we are historically sitting on centuries of Christian doctrine and dogma that has heavily influenced our relationship with life and death.

I want to add that I have no intention of pushing a belief in reincarnation (or any religious or spiritual belief come to that). Belief is such a personal thing. Nevertheless, I am fascinated by the possibility that I may have been here before and may well come back again. It makes me really appreciate how unique this lifetime is, and how it sets the scene for other possible life experiences in the future.

I deeply respect those who do not share my fascination. Yet exploring different and sometimes challenging spiritual and religious views over the past thirty years has helped me to form and establish a profound faith that works for me. Those not drawn to exploring this historical overview may want to jump to the end of the next chapter and read the interview with Liz Bryan, educational consultant for St Christopher's Hospice.

CHAPTER 2

SALVATION IS THE ONLY WAY!

Many religious and spiritual teachings include those about reincarnation[8] or rebirth[9]. We mainly attribute these to eastern traditions such as Buddhism and Hinduism, but reincarnation also lies at the heart of Western esoteric teachings such as Theosophy, the writings of Alice Bailey, and religions such as Paganism and Shamanism. Many indigenous and tribal societies also believe in different forms of reincarnation or rebirth.

It is said that ancient Greek philosophers such as Pythagoras, Socrates and Plato vigorously discussed metempsychosis – the migration of the soul. One of the earliest accounts of reincarnation is recorded in Plato's Myth of Er (c.428-347 BCE). A man named Er died in a battle and his body was placed on a funeral pyre. Suddenly he came back to life and recounted a story of visiting the afterlife where he learned about reincarnation, the celestial spheres, and how the good are rewarded and the bad are punished. This story greatly influenced religious and philosophical thought for centuries.

Several pieces of evidence contained in the Dead Sea Scrolls, found in a cave on northwest shore of the Dead Sea in 1954, suggests that early Judeo-Christian teachings included those about reincarnation[10]. However, it is said that references to reincarnation in the old and new testaments were removed during the Second Council of Constantinople in A.D. 553[11]. This council, consisting of 153 bishops, was summoned by Emperor Justinian to debate, clarify and edit a multitude of early Christian doctrines into a manageable authoritative scripture, or biblical canon.

Thus continued the removal of many scrolls and texts, including Mary's Gospel (considered by many to be Mary Magdalene rather than Mary, mother of Jesus) which represented the Divine Feminine[12]. These banished scrolls and texts are referred to as the Gnostic Gospels or the Lost Gospels which are said to contain mystical or esoteric knowledge about connecting directly with the Divine (considered unacceptable and heretical by the burgeoning early Church)[13].

It was also decided that if people continued to believe in reincarnation it would pose a threat to the power of the Church as being the only route to salvation. Therefore, belief in reincarnation was declared as heresy, and although the tenet of 'what you sow, so shall you reap' remained throughout the Bible, 'reincarnation' became absorbed into resurrection from the dead. The Church considered that only someone as ascended as Jesus could either create a miracle (raising Lazarus from the dead) or perform it himself when he appeared as the risen Christ to Mary Magdalene after his crucifixion. However, the Bible is peppered with references to reincarnation, for example, Jesus says that Elijah 'was born again as John the Baptist.' And many Christians across the globe are waiting for the second coming of Christ.

Even so, over centuries the Church's rebuff of reincarnation became entrenched in the collective Christian psyche and passed on from generation to generation (I should add that conventional Judaism and Islam – both monotheist religions – mainly refute reincarnation, although there is a precept of orthodox Judaism which calls the concept of reincarnation *gilgul* or *ha'atakah*. The mystic traditions of the Kabbala, Sufism and Christian Mysticism are much more open to it).

Eastern spiritual traditions such as Hinduism and Buddhism, which date back to around 2300 BCE and 600 BCE respectively, were never influenced by the early Church's emerging doctrines. Therefore, Eastern concepts about reincarnation and rebirth have continued for thousands of years.

Early English Church

Although Christianity was already present in Britain, the first push to convert the throng of warring kingdoms happened in 595 when Pope Gregory I sent a Roman monk called Augustine (later to be known as Augustine of Canterbury or St Augustine) as a missionary to England.

Following Augustine's conversion of King Ethelbert of Kent, Christianity began to slowly spread to other parts of the country forcing our ancient ancestors to give up their many gods and worship of the natural world. Their sacred Pagan sites and temples were increasingly turned into Christian places of worship and Pagan festivals were adopted into the Christian calendar. People could now only access God through the intermediary of holy representatives such as monks and friars. Their Pagan creator god transformed into an external force who had fashioned the world and had the power to look into the darkest recesses of their heart. Salvation from sin was granted only through Jesus Christ, the Redeemer.

William the Conqueror who became King of England in 1066 was a devout Christian. After he conquered the country, he did what he could to spread the Christian religion throughout England.

From the fifth century, the Church conducted services and sacraments from the Bible written in Latin. Most people were illiterate and would never have seen a book or had any knowledge of Latin. But with little choice, they succumbed to being told how to think, how to behave, how to pray, and how to die. Throughout Europe, those who challenged the Church or continued to work with the old ways were accused of heresy or witchcraft and were either burnt, hung or beheaded.

The Ars Moriendi

During these early times, death happened on a vast scale often due to war and terrible diseases such as the Black Death. But this meant that priests either couldn't reach the dying person in time or were too terrified to get close to them or were dead themselves. Therefore, a surviving family member or friend had to step in to offer the last rites. To make sure the Church's teachings were followed by these lay people, the Vatican created *Ars Moriendi* (Ars, 'skill' or 'craft', Moriendi 'of dying'): *The Art of Dying.*

Traditionally, *Ars Moriendi* consisted of 11 woodcuts (sometimes accompanied by text for those who could read) illustrating a dying man's struggle to overcome the five great temptations: unbelief, despair, impatience, pride and avarice. These vices were symbolised by devils surrounding the deathbed. On an opposing woodcut, a host of angels and other celestial forces rush to the dying man's side to support his struggle to overcome these evil forces. The woodcuts show the dying man resisting angelic help five times until the eleventh and final woodcut which shows the dying man finally accepting divine intervention and overcoming his sinful temptations.

The success of *Ars Moriendi* lay in the simple illustrations acting as a kind of teaching aid, cutting across the social classes. No matter their social status, everyone could reflect on the woodcuts and allow the images to convey the importance of redemption and true repentance.

The mass production of *Ars Moriendi* (made possible by William Claxton's invention of the printing press) meant that many more households in Europe had a copy. From an early age, children were encouraged to study it and absorb the reality that one-day they too, would fight for their salvation as they lay dying. In the meantime, *Ars Moriendi* reminded everyone of the importance of living an honest, fulfilling life as a preparation for entering purgatory after death (a kind of half-way house between earth and heaven) where they would have to atone for their sins before being admitted into heaven.

The Reformation

By the 16th century the Church was procuring enormous amounts of money from their communicants through the sale of Papal Indulgence, which promised to speed up time in purgatory for the dead and guaranteed the living exemption from punishment or penance for certain types of sin.

People knew about this corruption but were too terrified to speak out until Martin Luther rebelled in 1517. Luther, a German theologian, priest and monk, argued that the Bible, not the Church, was the only infallible authority on how a person might enter the Kingdom of Heaven and salvation could only be received through faith in Jesus Christ, the Savior.

Luther gained a huge following, and his writings circulated widely, soon finding their way to England. Although King Henry VIII remained theologically close to Catholicism, he leaned on Luther's reformation ideals to support his quest to divorce his catholic wife Catherine of Aragon and marry Anne Boleyn, who expressed a keen interest in Luther's ideas. And so, the Reformation and dissolution of the monasteries began, and the Protestant Church of England was born.

During the subsequent reign of Elizabeth 1, the whole idea of purgatory, rites, rituals, prayers for the dead and communication with those in the afterlife, were swept away by the new Protestant faith. This 'Protestantism' was much more existential, declaring that the fate of the soul was sealed at the moment of death (not after death), and people were to be judged only by the manner in which they had lived their life. Anyone who continued to follow the old Catholic faith of praying for the dead, talking to the dead, or believing in purgatory was declared a heretic. It must have been incredibly confusing and frightening for many simple, uneducated people who practiced the old faith and had no idea of what these changes meant apart from the fact it was heresy to deny them. The baton of religious faith kept passing violently between Catholicism and Protestant doctrine until King James I, a life-long Protestant, finally established Protestant England.

Nature becomes a commodity

The popularity of the *Ars Moriendi* was already beginning to fade when French philosopher Rene Descartes re-introduced critical questioning during the 1700s. This gave rise to a much more rational and intellectual approach to life which created a split between mind (religion) and matter (science) and laid the foundation for the Age of Enlightenment.

What followed was an explosion of controversial biological observations and geological discoveries about the natural world which challenged the Church's doctrine that life on Earth had come into being as a result of divine creation. This culminated in Charles Darwin's theory of evolution, which focused on competition and survival of the fittest. His theory contributed to our changing relationship with the natural world (which, in fact, started tens of thousands of years ago when humans evolved from being hunter-gathers to Neolithic and, later, Stone Age farmers) as a sacred and divine creation to one of 'man against nature.' Nature became increasingly regarded as a commodity to be exploited for the purposes of wealth, status and political influence.

Alongside scientific breakthroughs and innovations, medical practitioners started to take a more central role in what happened to the sick and how much a dying person should know about the end of life. In 1760, the English playwright and politician Richard Sheridan wrote; 'Very few people now die. Physicians take care to conceal people's danger from them. So, they are carried off, properly speaking, without dying: that is to say, without being sensible of it'.

Concealing 'people's dangers' has remained the status quo ever since. It's only recently that people have been calling for change and voicing a desire to take back control of how they die.

It took two world wars to stop people expressing grief in public. During World War One, the country was forced to face death on a massive scale. It was quickly realised that an entire population clothed in black not only destroyed public morale, it did not encourage young men to sign up for military service. As the war began in 1914, society magazines advocated the abandonment of mourning dress and in 1918 at the war's end, as Kate Berridge reported in her book *Vigor Mortis,* the Easter sermon delivered from the pulpit of St Paul's Cathedral in London requested the people 'cease this unseemly obsession with death'. After that, death and dying became a much more private affair and kept separate from the rituals of communal remembrance services.

New wonder drugs

During the Second World War significant advances were made in science and medicine and in 1944 Alexander Fleming was knighted for discovering penicillin. Named the new wonder drug, it saved thousands of soldiers from dying of wound infections.

The use of morphine was also widespread during both World Wars to ease excruciating pain caused by ballistic injuries and amputations. Other anaesthetic drugs such as meperidine were also developed to help combat the agony that so many men experienced from the terrible wounds they suffered.

These life-saving and pain-relieving treatments encouraging the sick and injured to increasingly turn away from spiritual comfort offered by priests and chaplains. Rather, patients regarded medicine as their God, and willingly handed over all decision-making about their treatment and the way they were informed (or not informed) about their illness to those who administered these wonder drugs; doctors.

With the focus on alleviating pain and extending life through the use of antibiotics and other life enhancing treatments, the sick and ailing were increasingly admitted into hospitals rather than dying at home.

However, the removal of death from the home meant that family members grew ignorant of what death looked like, what happens when someone started to die, or how to cope with the emotional intensity of sitting with someone who was dying.

Updated Government statistics for 2018 states that almost half of all deaths in England (46.9% – although I believe its higher than this) occur in hospital. This precedent has continued to the present day.

The sixties revolution

The cultural revolution of the sixties changed our relationship with life and death yet again. The young lost faith in the establishment and turned away from political governance and religious doctrines. Most wanted something new and exciting, and many, similar to the Beatles, became inspired by Eastern spiritual practices such as Transcendental Meditation (TM), which introduced them to altered states of consciousness, reincarnation and rebirth, and the concept of karma. Many others turned to psychedelic drugs and smoked pot to access higher states of being. The establishment denounced this as reckless and wacky. And, it certainly was a wild time. I clearly remember the American psychologist Timothy Leary urging us to 'turn on, tune in, and drop out.'

The 1960s gave birth to the New Age. But there is very little new about the New Age. At the same time as morphing into a multi-billion-dollar industry, New Age thinking is simply repackaged ancient mystical teachings and Eastern spiritual practices for our Western linear minds to understand.

At the same time that many of us were getting high in the sixties and seventies, death was being shunned.

In short, people didn't just stop talking about death and dying, they turned it into a taboo. Dr Elisabeth Kubler-Ross was one of the first medical professionals in the 1970s to write about her dismay at how death had become a 'dreaded and unspeakable issue to be avoided by any means possible in modern society.'

Slow process of change

It's been a slow process of change since Elisabeth Kubler-Ross wrote about her dismay, and I find it really sad that 40 years on we in the UK continue to struggle to talk openly and honestly about death and dying.

Although the UK hospice movement, set up by Dame Cicely Saunders in 1967, is regarded as the best in the world for providing spiritual care for the dying, the care that dying people and their families receive in National Health hospitals (and in many care homes) continues to raise the most complaints. This is mainly because hospitals are places (in theory) that help people to get well, and it's still relatively unusual for nurses and doctors to receive specialist training to provide end of life care or talk about end of life issues or spiritual matters. It creates a difficult dynamic between the patient who may want to know the truth and medical staff who find it uncomfortable to tell the truth.

Liz Bryan is an educational consultant for St Christopher's Hospice. She is well aware of the issues that we all can face at the end of life.

I believe most people are afraid of death because they don't think about it. We live in a society where we expect everything to be convenient and easy, and we don't expect human life to be traumatic. But when our well-worn strategies fail, we have no idea how to defend ourselves against pain and suffering.

We don't prepare or teach our children about pain and suffering either. This means that many of us grow up relationally incompetent and will do anything to avoid conflict or difficult emotions. For example, we would rather get divorced these days than work things through. It also means we have no idea how to enter the transition of what it means to let go, and to consciously engage in the very real grief of endings. This doesn't just have to be about the death of someone we love or our own death, it could be any major change in our life such as our children leaving home, the menopause, or looking into the mirror as we age, wondering 'Where have I gone?'

Working through endings which happen in our lives teaches us wisdom, self-awareness, emotional maturity, and what good listening means. Most people have no idea that listening is much more than just hearing words.

It also prepares us to understand that suffering is a part of life, and we are not alone. So many people believe that there is something wrong with them because they are going through a difficult time and can't cope, and they believe they are the only one to experience it. I find that really sad.

In my eleven years working with St Christopher's I have seen many people entering the final stage of life. I am very aware of how people who have lived with conflict or have had complex relationships can struggle emotionally. But I have certainly witnessed very touching healing of relationships which has helped the dying person to find a sense of peace. This is why I respect the hospice philosophy or model. I look at it as a way of being that offers people a safe place to therapeutically do whatever they need to do to help them let go. It's sad that this model is difficult to create in other settings such as in hospitals and even at home. We really do need to understand that dying is far more than just managing physical symptoms. It is equally important to address our spiritual welfare.

How do I want to die, personally? I would like to die at home, preferably with my family around me. But it is up to them whether they want to be present or not. The most important thing for me is that everyone knows they are loved, and everything that needs to be said or done has happened. I would also like to know about anything I have done or said or the way I have behaved that has caused conflict or tension. I would like to apologise for it.

I am also clear about who else I want with me. My best friend has already agreed to be with me (assuming I die before her) and I know she will do everything she can to look after and protect my children and my husband. That gives me great comfort. I would also like medication if I begin to feel distressed or I become breathless. I don't want to die in pain.

In the next chapter we are going to explore why fearing death makes us afraid of life, and how the psychological impact of our childhood conditioning influences our ability to live fully and die consciously.

CHAPTER 3

WHY ARE WE SO AFRAID OF LIVING?

Whether we believe in God or not, our Western culture is sitting on centuries of cultural, political, colonial and religious doctrine which has programmed our collective psyche with a deep sense of separateness or duality (living in a world of opposites). Ask a native American Indian where God is, they will point to their heart. Ask a Westerner, they point to the sky.

This separation (so alien to spiritual wellbeing) drives us to look outside ourselves for something to attach to in order for us to feel safe. We search desperately and endlessly to find other people or 'things' to make life right for us: the right spouse; the right phone; the right job; the right school; the right house in the right area; the right pair of designer shoes and the right car. Our desire for 'the right life' creates in us a voracious hunger engaged in the impossible pursuit of physical immortality. Or it might be status and fame that we crave to make us whole. Or we become spiritual seekers, endlessly searching for the meaning of life.

Yet, people who accept their mortality develop a healthy relationship with both life and death. They carry a sense of inner knowing and calmness – and a deep understanding about the absurdity of life. Therefore, accepting mortality is not about giving up or sacrificing who we are. It's about finding out who we are.

One of the most powerful ways to break through our fear of life is to understand that death is not an end to life. Life itself, cannot and does not 'end.' Nor can life be destroyed. Quantum physics provides compelling data that life is an energetic force found throughout the Universe and is present in every facet of the natural world. Therefore, death of the physical body is, in fact, a completion of life in one form and the transition of life into another energetic form. Yet, most of us in our Western cultures are led to believe that life is a one-stop shop and then we fall off the end of the conveyor belt. We are also told that speaking about death is morbid, depressing and anxiety-making. It's no wonder we find living and dying daunting. So, let's explore our relationship with living and dying in more detail.

The goal of life is to die

'The goal of life is to die,' stated Sigmund Freud, the father of psychoanalysis. He considered that human beings possess an unconscious desire to die but our survival instincts largely alleviate this wish. Therefore, death and life are constantly rubbing up against the each other, creating an unconscious inner tension until we psychologically learn to make peace with the fact that to be alive means we will die.

But there is more to add to the mix. We have created a society where most of us are born into the rigors of the human condition without a clue about the rules or anyone to explain them to us. We may go to school but most of us leave devoid of any life skills to deal with what lies ahead. As a result, we end up learning about life through experiencing pain, suffering, grief and despair. We have frightening or terrifying experiences. We feel guilt, shame, self-doubt and self-hate. We hurt ourselves just as we hurt others whether intentionally or not. We experience loneliness, isolation and separation, and a sense of yearning for something we can't find. In spite of this, we begin to realise the human journey is also about healing, joy and happiness, finding love and connection, meaning, purpose, wellbeing and wholeness. But it's hard to establish this side of the coin when we've never been taught to respect and love ourselves. Some of us hit lucky with love. Others end up swimming around in thick soup despairing about what's gone wrong.

Even so, there seems to be a deep psychological need in all of us to make sense of what it means to be human. But why?

The most convincing answer I have come across is from Socrates, the Greek classical philosopher who lived 399 BC. He said,' The proper practice of philosophy is 'about nothing else but dying and being dead.'

I think he's right. Although most of us are unaware of it, from the moment we are born, our entire lives are spent psychologically preparing for when our end comes. Every challenge and crisis pushes us back on ourselves and tests our beliefs and faith (if we have a faith) to the limit. This tension gives rise to the three most important questions we will ever ask ourselves: 'Who am I am?' 'Why am I here?' 'What's the point of my life?'

However, our overly stimulated, highly competitive and aggressive Western society does not encourage profound reflection. Rather, we pack our heads with layer upon layer of information, knowledge and facts, with little ability to turn it into the wisdom and connectedness of spiritual wellbeing.

This means we live in our heads as we logically try to work out the best way to survive. It comes at a price. When we defer to critical thinking, we lose the ability to listen to our inner voice which helps us to make informed, balanced judgements and decisions that nurture and support our life. Instead, we end up scared of change, terrified of failure, and petrified of losing control. This feeds our fear of life, and ultimately our fear of death.

What can we do to change this?

The answer is that we need to confront any psychological blocks that stand in the way of developing spiritual wellbeing. This can be painful and challenging but we have to do this profound inner work if we want to engage with what it means to live fully and die consciously. The path to spiritual wellbeing is about making the choice to do this work.

None of us are victims to life or death

We are all scared by life, some of us more than others. Nevertheless, I believe that none of us are victims to it. Each one of us is filled with potential and our job is to tap into this potential so we can break through what is holding us back from becoming a successful human being. The American poet and philosopher Ralph Waldo Emerson sums up beautifully what a successful human being is by saying, 'To leave the world a bit better, whether by a healthy child, a garden patch, or redeemed social condition; to know even one life has breathed easier because you live—that is to have succeeded.'

People who quietly recognise the contributions they have made to the world are much more at peace with themselves and they take this peace into death. I believe we can all achieve this state of grace, but first we need to make room inside ourselves for a state of grace to arise. For this to happen, we need to start at the beginning by understanding how our childhood conditioning affects the way we think about ourselves.

We are born to connect

Unconditional love is the most powerful gift any parent can give their child. It teaches us healthy attachment, to be proud of who we are, and makes us feel safe as we grow and develop into adults. Conversely, when we are not unconditionally loved as infants, it breeds self-doubt, fear and low self-worth. I am conscious as I write this about the impact that my own parenting has had on my two sons. But healing is about addressing and owning our deepest wounds so we can change how we relate to ourselves and those we love.

'Give me the boy until he is seven, and I will give you the man,' said Aristotle more than two thousand years ago. He was right. During the 1950s and 1960s psychologists and psychiatrists such as Edward Bowlby and Melanie Klein recognised that as young children, we have an inherent psychological need and desire to connect to our main primary care-giver, and this relationship is crucial during our first five years into order for us to mature healthily into adulthood. Bowlby believed that when this primary relationship is disrupted or doesn't happen at all, our ability to psychologically grow into rounded individuals is impaired.

Professor Allan Schore is an American psychologist and world leading researcher in the field of neuropsychology in infants. He conducts studies on brain development in children that builds on Bowlby's attachment theory. He says we are born with our brain's neurological networks physiologically programmed to connect to our mother or whoever is our primary caregiver. This connection, he says, gives us a sense of belonging, safety, and identity, and even at an early age, we store in our bodies everything that goes on in our lives. Babies, he states, are unable to control their emotions. It is the job of the mother by her own thoughts and actions to show the baby how emotions [such as love] can be healthily expressed[14].

According to Schore, when we fail to connect to our mother as new borns, high levels of stress hormones are released into our nervous system which affects the way our infant brain physiologically develops during childhood, and in turn, how we are able to form trusting and loving relationships as we grow into adults. Therefore, those of us who experience emotional or physical disconnection or abuse or neglect during our early years will often struggle to develop a true sense of self. This creates emotional turmoil, which drastically affects our relationship as adults with living and dying.

Childhood conditioning

Although many of us are fortunate to be brought up in stable loving homes we, as young children, quickly realise that the strength and constancy of our parents' love depends on how we conform to what they and our wider community consider as the 'norm.' Therefore, we begin to live through the filter of our parental conditioning and society's expectations. How many of us swore to ourselves during our childhood and adolescence that we would NEVER become like our parents? Then years later we catch ourselves speaking in the same tone and manner or adopting the same behaviour.

This happens because of our organic need for deep connection and belonging from birth. However, as young vulnerable children we can easily feel disconnected by experiencing for example, a parent's disapproval, ridicule or over-indulgence (lack of boundaries makes a child feel unsafe and uncontained). Sometimes our parents are too busy to pay us any attention or they may have high expectations that can't be met. Or we might be subjected to physical, emotional, mental or sexual threat, or actual abuse and violence. This breeds an acute shame that there is something wrong with us.

There is another layer to consider. Many parents are unconsciously carrying unresolved generational trauma which they pass onto their offspring. This is why some predispositions such as alcoholism, gambling and abuse or certain physical conditions can be traced back through the family tree. Yet, this does not mean that these predispositions are set in stone. We can all choose to do things differently by healing ourselves. In doing so we also energetically heal the wounds of our ancestors.[15] We will be revisiting this in Section 3.

The world can appear to be a hostile, isolating place until we start the healing process. To survive we often work out a false persona to obtain the love and connection we crave, or at least to get noticed. The origin of the word 'person' comes from the Latin *Persona*, meaning an actor's mask or a character in a play. Carl Jung, who founded analytical psychology, was the first psychiatrist to use the concept of persona to differentiate between our 'I'-personality (our face or mask to the world) and our authentic, genuine 'Me' inner self.

'I' and 'Me'

I understand the true role of our 'I'-personality (some refer to this as the ego) as our own unique human expression made possible through the physical body. It is how we express ourselves in life. Our authentic inner 'Me' experiences, connects and integrates with the physical world through our 'I'- personality. In other words, our inner 'Me' expresses through the physical individuality of our 'I'. Once this particular life is over, the 'I'- personality's job is done and I believe it dies along with our body. Consequently, to my way of thinking, it is the 'I'-personality which holds our fear of death.

The inner authentic 'Me' is connected to a far higher source of consciousness and spiritual evolution and is therefore essentially eternal. Spiritual wellbeing is created when there is free flow between our 'I'-personality and our authentic inner 'Me' and peace comes to us at the end of our life when we relinquish our earthbound 'I'-personality and turn to this higher 'Me 'consciousness.

When this free flow is absent, it causes a split between 'I' and 'Me'. Rather, the 'I'-personality persona (face or mask to the world) we adopt becomes the dominant force of how we express ourselves in the world. In order to survive, our persona needs to identify and relate with the external world. When we are not in harmony with our inner Me, our 'I'-personality takes over and *becomes* an outward expression of our beliefs, moods, attitudes, traumas and opinions which smothers our ability to connect with our inner 'Me'. Such discord stops us from feeling safe in our body. We feel as if we are hovering just outside it or living half in and half out of it. This disconnect from our body shows itself in some form of physical or mental ill health. An essential part of healing into spiritual wellbeing is to find ways to fully incarnate into the body so we can become present with who we are.

So, how do we adopt these personas and, more important, how can we begin to engage with spiritual wellbeing to harmonise the split between 'I' and 'Me'?

Expecting to conform

I consider we develop our persona in three ways: **We adopt our parent/parents' behaviour and become like them** (appeasing to win love). We have an inherent need to connect, fit in and feel safe, so we adopt, for example, their personality and tone of voice. Or we create roles that are acceptable to them. For example, we become the clown in the family, or the clever academic, the performer, the carer (mother's little helper), the peacemaker, the fighter, or, perhaps, even the black sheep. There are lots of roles we can adopt to try and win our parents' approval or get noticed. A common theme is entering the same work or career path of a parent even though we don't want to but feel the intensity of expectation. Or we take on their illnesses, traumas, addictive habits and unresolved grief and shame.

We would rather die than be like our parents (rebelling). For those of us who survive by becoming rebels, we welcome double trouble. We yearn for connection but as we do not resonate with the way we are being parented or with our parents values, we cut ourselves off from them, believing we know best. We reject both good and bad that our parents offer and stop ourselves from listening to anything that threatens this rebellious identity. Many of us leave home at an early age. Yet, without the wisdom or maturity to make informed choices, or the ability to listen, we end up raging against what we perceive to be an unjust, unloving world and often find ourselves ostracised on fringes of society. It's an isolating place to be, yet it takes a lot for the rebel to turn this around because, after all, a rebel knows best.

We develop ambivalence towards our parent/ parents (we want to please them, but don't want to be like them). This makes us confused about our feelings for them, so we keep our distance, or we withdraw our love or hide it away deep inside. Many of us experience ambivalence when our parent has not matured emotionally and is incapable of caring for us as a healthy adult. We end up feeling responsible for parenting them, often a very early age. This makes us feel resentful, angry and shamed without fully understanding why.

Further turmoil is created because we usually feel differently towards each of our parents and bond more strongly with one parent than the other. For example, we may adopt our mother's behaviour to become like her, and at the same time rebel against our father. Or we may feel ambivalent towards our father and rebel against our mother. Or we can over identify with the emotional needs of one parent, especially a single parent, so we become more like a partner (appeasing) to them than their child. This can add to our emotional confusion and set up yet more conflict within in the already tenuous relationship and within ourselves.

Pretending to be someone else

Whether we become appeasers, rebels, or develop ambivalence towards one or both parents we hide behind the persona or façade we have developed, pretending we are someone else as we try to negotiate our way through childhood into adulthood.

Consequently, many of us reach adolescence unable to relate to the world with any sense of authenticity.

It makes us feel lonely, isolated and ashamed, with no idea that the purpose of life is to learn what it means to be a human being who is here to evolve in wisdom and spiritual wellbeing. Instead, we shut down even further. But the more we shut down the more we feel out of control of our life, which distorts our relationship with death. In some cases, this can manifest as death phobia, death denial, death obsession (the Goth movement), death envy (wishing it was you when you hear someone else has died) or believing that suicide is the only way out. This is what Rebecca experienced. Rebecca is now in her late forties and a working mother. She told me how the impact of her very dysfunctional childhood drove her to attempt to take her own life.

Both my parents were very dysfunctional. In fact, my mother ended up marrying my father's brother after my father left home. There was a lot of threat and violence going on between them, and this led to a lot of confusion and shame for me. When my mother finally went, she left a note on the table saying she'd gone shopping and she never returned. She phoned me in the evening to ask me to tell my stepfather. Ever heard of 'shoot the messenger?' Well, that's exactly what happened to me. He went ballistic. He then went back to his parents and I had to take care of myself with no money. I was sixteen at the time. Looking back, I am not surprised I attempted suicide. I wanted someone to recognise what a mess I was in. I realise now that I didn't want to die. I just wanted my situation to die. I was so lucky to have a friend who found me and took me to her house. I needed that unconditional love and a place of safety to pick myself up again. It helped me to remember that even though I believed I was broken on some level I was whole on another. That's what I clung to, and that's what got me through. Today, when I look at my daughter, I am so proud of her, and my ability to provide her with a stable home so she can blossom in the way I never could. I know I have made something of my life because of her. I can die at peace now.

Coming back to who you are

Spiritual wellbeing begins when we ask ourselves questions such as, 'Am I living my own life or someone else's?' 'Am I really thinking this, or is this the voice of my mother/father (or anyone else who had a strong influence over you, whether good or bad)?' 'Do I want to do this, or am I doing it because I am expected to?' 'Who the hell am I?' One workshop participant said, 'I know what I think isn't ME. I feel as if my mother is living in my head.' Another participant described her life as, 'I feel as if I am living in a box which doesn't have my name on it.' Yet another said, 'I just seem to be chasing after life, but not catching up with it.'

Belinda is a family therapist in her early fifties (she preferred not to give her real name). She spoke to me about how she finally broke out of the box she found herself in, and how this inspired her to help other people to do the same.

I was close to my father but very ambivalent towards my mother. My mother was more like a child. I spent a lot of time supporting her and being her counsellor, I suppose. That was the façade I developed. The carer. I wanted to take away her pain so our family could be well. All I really wanted to do was to sing, but the message from both my parents was, 'that isn't a proper job.' So, I never developed the confidence to even try.

I ended up in the caring profession because of looking after my mother. I realise now she carried a lot of trauma from how her own mother had treated her. But she passed this trauma on to my brother and me. She suffered from a lot of fear and anxiety and illnesses. I developed illnesses and depression as well. It took until mid-life to realise I had no idea who I was.

Going into therapy helped me to understand that I had split off parts of myself in order to survive. These traumatised parts had literally hidden the healthy parts on me. Looking at the bigger picture helped me to build up self-esteem for the first time, and I stopped feeling so alone. Although I am still very much working on myself, I am no longer overwhelmed by life. I know when I am being authentic, and I learnt not to accept jobs that I am in conflict with. Creating conflict erodes away well-being.

The key was learning to read the messages my body was giving me, rather than living in my head. I now do systemic family work, which helps people to understand who they truly are. Although it's challenging, I find this work a joy. I believe you have to discover who you really are. It's essential because you can't run away from yourself. You certainly can't run away from yourself when you are on your deathbed. So, you might as well find out who you are while you are alive. Knowing this makes me feel resilient and courageous. People need to stop and think what life means to them and to become conscious about what they want to do. It's about developing discernment. My journey began when I starting to ask myself 'Why am I so afraid of life? Why am I terrified to shine?' Yes, I am still a work in progress, but if I died now, I believe I would be proud of myself. So, in that sense, death has lost its fear.

To generate the resilience and courage that Belinda speaks of, we need to develop emotional intelligence. Therefore, in the second section of the book we will be looking at the psychology of living fully and dying consciously and how we can develop a healthier relationship with our mortality.

THE PSYCHOLOGY OF DYING CONSCIOUSLY

CHAPTER 4

FACING THE TIGER

Spiritual wellbeing deepens when we ask ourselves, 'Do I want to take how I feel about myself to my deathbed?' If the answer is yes, then we are doing really well. If the answer is 'No,' it's our cue to do things differently. To do things differently, we need to find ways to shed the false persona we have adopted.

This can be very challenging. However, when I began to grasp a deeper understanding of the human condition and what it means to integrate body, mind and soul, I stopped feeling crushed by life. I also began to find ways to gain control over my emotions and feelings. Rampaging feelings are like ferocious tigers, ready to pounce and kill at any moment They destroy our equilibrium and make us behave in ways which shame us. Therefore, an essential part of making peace with our mortality is about developing emotional intelligence.

We develop emotional intelligence by becoming mindful of what emotions or feelings are arising in the moment and learning to *pause* before we react. There's a lot to be said for taking a breath and counting up to ten to stop an argument escalating. It's much more powerful to consciously hold our counsel than try to win the fight. This does not mean we become a doormat to other people's opinions, criticisms or judgements. Nor does it mean running away from what is happening. It's about actively choosing whether it is in our best interests to engage or not. This helps us go beyond the drama and allows our inner 'Me' to guide us through those difficult moments.

The art of responding

There is also an art to responding to criticism with grace. I know how hard it is to hear the honest truth about myself. But sometimes we need to hear it so we can become more conscious of the way we impact on those around us. Emotional intelligence is about being open and receptive. Personally, I believe 'if the mud sticks,' it's time to listen, which means that when we have a strong reaction to someone's feedback, we may need to pay attention. When truth deepens, life changes.

The more we can gain control over our emotions and feelings the more we develop a sense of inner strength, safety and authenticity. We are not afraid to admit we are wrong, or to say sorry when it is appropriate. Or to tap someone on the shoulder to let them know that something isn't working for us. This authenticity automatically ripples out into all our personal relationships and into our acceptance of life and death.

Emotional intelligence helps us to settle into the life we are meant to live and enables us to become a good friend to ourselves. This allows us to approach our death feeling in control of what is going on around us, supports us in making informed choices of how we want to die and how we express our choices clearly to our family and those providing our end of life care.

So, how do we develop emotional intelligence? Let's start with exploring the difference between emotions and feelings.

Emotions vs feelings

Most people think that emotions and feelings are the same. In my understanding, they have different qualities.

Emotions are instinctual primary reactions *to* events that happen to us. They surface *first* and we have *no control over them*. Sometimes we can have such a strong reaction that we are flooded by our primary emotion and it takes time to see clearly again.

Feelings are triggered *by* the event. In other words, they arise in our body *in response to the event,* governed by our subconscious learnt behaviours, personal experiences, conditioning, beliefs and memories that can stretch way back to childhood. Our brain is constantly trying to make sense of what is happening to us. Therefore, these secondary feelings give meaning and context to whatever primary emotion we experience. To give two simple examples: I unexpectedly win award. I experience the primary emotion of surprise. I then feel joy. I celebrate with friends. Or, my boyfriend unexpectedly ends the relationship. I experience the primary emotion of shock. Then feelings of grief and loss surface as visceral sensations in my body. I enter my grieving process.

As I have already mentioned, our feelings are complex and multi-layered, and dependent on our personal perceptions and experiences of life. Therefore, our secondary feelings are powerful signposts for the work we need to do on ourselves. To give another example, someone barges in front of us in a queue. We experience the primary emotion of anger, which is appropriate in the moment. But secondary feelings of low self-worth and fear push our anger aside. We were brought up never to make a fuss. So, we stay invisible and small and sit on our anger, letting it fester just as we have all our life.

Therefore, emotional intelligence and spiritual wellbeing are, for me, about deeply listening to what is going on inside, what feelings or sensations are arising in the body, and taking responsibility for what's happening *in the moment*. Some people regard self-awareness as self-obsession or selfishness. My answer to this is that when we unpack our pain and trauma, we release our fear of dying.

Once we understand how our feelings are only feelings and are *not* who we are, we can begin to form a far healthier relationship with life and death. This profound work enables us to go beyond our limitations so we can spend the rest of our life contributing positively and consciously to a world which is in desperate need of clarity, vision and wisdom. And, to remember that we are all in this soup of life together.

The Big Six

One of the main blocks to emotional intelligence and spiritual wellbeing is fear and anxiety. Therefore, the following section looks at the impact of what I consider to be The Big Six which drive fear and anxiety. Guilt and shame. Grief and loss. Anger and rage.

Guilt and shame

Guilt and shame are both self-conscious, self-blaming feelings. However, there is a distinct difference between the two. Guilt is *I have DONE something wrong* (I can try to put this right). Shame is *I AM wrong* (I am fundamentally flawed or broken).

Guilt

Guilt is believing 'I have done something wrong' even when it's not perceived by the other person or people as a wrongful act. We can feel guilty when we fail to do something that we believe is expected of us or we say harsh words with the intention to hurt someone. Or when we run away from a difficult situation, walk out of a relationship, face a moral dilemma, or when we are incapable of giving love to someone. We can feel guilty when we believe we have let someone down, or we kill or harm animals or damage the natural world. We can feel guilty when we steal property or withhold information or hold onto secrets. We feel guilt when we cause a fatal accident or serious injury, or when we inadvertently break someone else's possession.

The language of guilt goes along the lines of 'I am guilt ridden. I did something bad/awful. I am eaten up with guilt. I wish it had never happened. I would do anything to put it right. If only I could turn the clock back.'

However, guilt is part of the human condition which enables us to know right from wrong. When we own up to our guilt, however challenging or distressing the situation and whatever the outcome, we feel a sense of relief and release. It makes us humble. Humility helps us to learn from our mistakes and to mature emotionally and spiritually. It's healthy to feel remorseful because it reminds us that we are not 'God.' We learn to develop compassion for our own human failings and flaws and begin to realise that, in any given moment, everyone else is doing the best they can with who they are, just as we are.

Shame

Shame is far more complex because it's toxic. It makes us believe, 'I am fatally flawed and beyond help.' Shame is caused by intensely painful feelings that happen when we are driven by someone else to do something that creates self-disgust. This can be through bullying, religious dogma which programmes us to believe we are sinful, and acts that cause humiliation, embarrassment or abuse. For a child, any threat of abuse turns life into one of dread. To survive we often take on the shame of the abuser, which means we believe we are responsible for what is happening to us. But at the same time, we believe that if this is happening to me, there must be something wrong with me.

The sense of being damaged, broken or fatally flawed is so overwhelming and painful that it becomes all consuming. To escape, we cover up the pain through distorted behaviours and disorders. For example, we start idealising other people, believing they are perfect (our celebrity culture is an example). Or we become obsessively jealous about those we believe to have what we don't. Or we take vindictive pleasure in shaming others to escape our own feelings of shame. Therefore, shame can make us narcissistic, self-righteous, ego-centric, vain and self-obsessed.

The language of shame is, 'I am broken. I hate myself. I am disgusting. I am dirty. I am worthless. I am an imposter. If anyone really knew what I was like, they would hate me.' Therefore, we keep our shame a secret. But this turns our shame into an identity rather than a feeling, making us terrified of being found out.

It's important to understand that although we are born with the capacity to feel guilt (to know right from wrong) we are *not* born with shame. A friend who stayed with the indigenous Shaur people of South America[16] told me she was astonished to learn they do not possess a word for 'shame.' It simply does not exist in their language. However, back in the West our psyches have been impregnated by centuries of religious doctrine that tells us we are sinful and bad. Even though many of us have turned our backs on such religious dogma, it is hard to shake off.

The most tragic impact of shame is that it cuts off our ability to engage with life and death or to experience spiritual wellbeing. Rather, it stalks us day and night, lashing out at us without warning with those shame attacks that make us cringe and want to hide away. I have worked with a number of clients who say they are literally 'dying of shame.'

Speak out!

John Bradford, author of *Healing the Inner Child*, says we are only sick as our secrets, and the only way out of our shame is to have the courage to speak about it. If we don't trust anyone, he advises us to tell it to the shower curtain or to the plant in the pot, the dog or the cat. The act of speaking it out loud means it is no longer remains an unspoken secret.

Certainly, as Elisabeth Kubler-Ross writes about in her book, *On Death and Dying*, many people who hold onto unexpressed guilt and shame become increasingly agitated and find it difficult to let go. I experienced this with my own mother. She was a very private person, but I was aware that she was full of shame and guilt about her own mother. Maybe it was because she came from a generation who rarely spoke about their feelings that she chose not to talk to anyone about it. I believe this lay at the root of the chronic health conditions she suffered for years. I was with her as she lay dying, often crying out in anxiety and distress. There was nothing I could do but sit with her. I was very relieved for her when she finally died.

Conversely, many end-of-life studies show that when dying people are helped to speak about their shame and guilt, possibly for the first time, it is as if they have been liberated from an internal prison and can finally die with serenity. But, how sad to leave it until we enter our dying process. I believe it is far better to face our fear while we have time to heal and enjoy life in a different way.

This is the choice that Rebecca has made. Rebecca is in her early forties. She is a mum and wife and works in the health industry.

I was brought up in a very dysfunctional, violent family. My brother became increasingly disturbed and used to pay me visits. I knew what he was doing to me was wrong, but I just felt his loneliness and desperation. It didn't make it okay, but it wasn't seedy – not like a creepy uncle fiddling with you. But I got to the point when I told him that if he carried on, I would tell Mum and Dad. It never happened again.

The impact it had on my childhood was monumental. I completely failed at school and my shame turned me into someone who was pissed all the time, constantly having suicidal thoughts and sleeping with anyone who took the faintest interest in me. It was crumbs from the table.

I realised that I was deeply traumatised by what had happened to me, but I thought trauma and PTSD [posttraumatic stress disorder] was only what soldiers got. It had nothing to do with me. I finally began to wake up when I fell down the stairs pissed again and was relieved that I had managed to save the wine bottle. I remember standing in front of the mirror when I 'heard' a male voice say, 'This is your life.' I thought it was God and I was overcome with such feelings of tragedy and profound guilt. I was smart and intelligent, but I was living a life of utter drama. I also realised that if we are already steeped in shame, we can only make decisions from a place of shame. That is incredibly self-destructive. This realisation led me onto my healing path.

What lies behind poor choices

Rebecca's comment, 'I also realised that if we are already steeped in shame, we can only make decisions from a place of shame,' is profoundly revealing. As I know myself, unresolved shame drives us to make destructive, ill-informed choices which are hard to come to terms with. Healing this shame is about learning to accept that the choices we made at the time came from a place of low self-worth, ignorance, fear and often undiagnosed depression. As much as we may wish it, we can't turn the clock back, but we can face up to our shame and learn from it. For me, my shame taught me about humility and how every choice I make in life has profound consequences for myself and those I love and how my life unfolds. This understanding pushed me into deep soul healing and the desire to work with people who also want to make peace with themselves.

I am particularly touched by Barbara's story. She is now in her late forties and teaches children to up to twelve years old. She told me of a shame she has carried since university days.

I was engaged to a white guy before I went to university. But when I got to university, I very quickly fell in love with a fellow student who was a black African. Within a few months I fell pregnant. I was terrified because I didn't know who the father of my baby was, and I kept thinking of what colour the baby might be. I wanted to be with my African boyfriend. I was madly in love with him. So, I broke off my engagement and had an abortion. I didn't want to do this, but I knew I had to, and I also realised I wasn't ready to have a baby at that stage of my life. I remember talking to the doctors before the abortion, but I had no idea about the impact the abortion would have on my life or how it would come back to haunt me when I had my own children. My African partner (who is the father of my children) knew about the abortion, but we never spoke about it. We just swept what happened under the carpet. The shame certainly impacted my relationship with my older child. Different forms of therapy have helped to lessen my guilt. I don't think about the baby every day, but the help I received has allowed the baby to remain my heart. I find that very comforting. Even so, I realise I have to live with the reality of what happened for the rest of my life.

Owning our painful experiences is vital for healing into spiritual wellbeing. We can't change the past, but we can learn to allow the grief and loss we experience to teach us about how to live a more connected and authentic life.

Grief and loss

Grief and loss do not come in nice neat packages. They rip our lives apart.

Yet, we all experience loss. It's part of the human condition. We experience loss through the death of someone we love either through illness or sudden or violent death. Or it may be having an abortion, a stillbirth, or our child dies. It may be the loss of a marriage, or a lover breaks our heart. Or perhaps it's the loss of a job, or facing retirement, or our children have left home to make their own way in the world. It may be learning to live with mental illness, chronic illness, when we are suddenly disabled, or we end up in prison. Or it could be when we look in the mirror one day and become overwhelmed by the loss of our youth. Or we become caught up in repeatedly regretting opportunities that we never took.

Sometimes losses rack up in a short space of time. One workshop participant spoke about her father dying and shortly afterwards, her best friend died. Then her cat died, and her husband left her. She said she felt she was being stalked by grief and loss.

Grief is the searing feelings that we experience when faced with loss and anything goes when grief pulverises the life out of us. For me, grief is like being thrown into a tumble dryer and I can't find the off switch. This is how workshop participants describe it: Despairing, angry, isolated, shame, guilt, martyrdom, deadness, total disconnection, regret, unsafe, vulnerable, bewildered, unsettled, relief, finite, dazed, lost, fractured, numb, sadness, stupid, unable to cope, ignorant, envious, falling apart, rage, heavy, going mad, loss of the future, complicated.

They describe loss as: Brokenness, pain, change, death of the old, powerlessness, change of identity, confusion, unknown, growth, out of control, ignorance, loss of identity, something gone missing, cheated, visceral in the body, heartbreak, resilience, not belonging, undigestible, alone, nostalgia, growth, buried, vulnerability, overwhelming, heaviness, betrayal, trivialised, violation, discovery of secrets (mistresses and other children can come to light) black dog, having to manage other people's feelings.

Society doesn't want to know

These chaotic, and often terrifying feelings need gentle care and love. But we live in a society which seems to be just as uncomfortable with grief and loss as it is with death and dying. One participant said, 'It [society] simply does not want to know. It's embarrassed, resistant, and makes assumptions. It wants to fix it rather than engage with it and treats grief as if it is a stigma or an illness.' Another participant said, 'We can't stay with the tears. We do anything we can to try and stop the other person from crying. There's no rituals to help us, and there's an entrenched expectation to 'Be Brave. Be strong.'

A Death Café participant spoke about how, as a teenager, she was never told that her mother was seriously ill. She knew something was wrong, but no one prepared her for what was happening. 'I was staying with a friend when she died. I had absolutely no idea. I was completely devastated but I never said a word and no one in the family spoke about Mum after the funeral. It's as if she had never existed. We all just got on with it. But I lost it. I started to fail at school and then I started to drink and take drugs. It was the only way I could cope with the immense pain I was carrying. This went on for years until I found help. But even now, I can connect with the pain of what it was like to feel so utter devastated. The repercussions never leave you.'

Another Death Café participant spoke about her brother who had died fifty-one years ago, and how her sister-in-law and family had never grieved for him. The participant said that recently her sister-in-law and niece had come for tea and both started to cry when she mentioned her long-dead brother. They had never spoken about him until that moment. The participant said to them, 'You should have done this crying fifty-one years ago when he died.'

Someone else spoke about the sudden death of a sibling. 'The whole family were having dinner together. It was a lovely evening. Everyone hugged each other when we said goodbye and that was the last time we saw her. She was killed on her way home. Just like that. Gone. She was only in her twenties. It completely fractured our family. My parents refused to talk about her, and we remaining siblings began to avoid each other. It took until both my parents died, for me to build up a relationship with my siblings again. Even now, twenty years on, they are uncomfortable talking about what happened. But I feel I need to talk about it. It helps.'

This is a sad reflection on how so many of us have been brought up to deny our grief and bury our sadness. Some of us actually believe that grief will kill us. In a sense it does until we start to process it.

Unprocessed grief makes us anxious, depressed, powerless and vulnerable. It seems as if something is missing – a hole which can't be filled. Some grieving people find it difficult to trust other people. Some become caught in the past, yearning for those 'better days', or have an irrational fear of entering into new relationships and of death itself. Others find themselves trapped in anger or rage or filling the gap through excessive 'doing.' Others survive by compartmentalising their lives or by appearing strong. One participant said that she dealt with her grief by exhausting herself into sleep.

Participants agree that life can never be the same again, and there's no magic potion for dealing with grief and loss. But all agree that grief and loss are powerful teachers.

What grief teaches us

Many bereaved people I have spoken to and worked with over the years have said that even though it was terrible at the time and deep sorrow still remains, they feel somehow that their lives have become enriched because of their experience of grief. For instance, some people feel compelled to start charities which help other people going through similar bereavements. Some turn to social justice issues, making the case for safety regulations or legislation to be changed, such as Helen's Law which is currently fighting to deny parole for murderers who refuse to reveal the location of their victims' bodies.

Some come to realise that life is precious, and completely change their lives by embracing adventures and experiences that would not have been possible before their bereavement. Some become more attuned to nature and far more concerned for the welfare of the planet.

Some speak about the freedom of realising they are not in control of what happens and have come to accept the unpredictability and impermanence of life. One workshop participant said that this taught her to stop planning ahead and she has learnt to become more present in the moment. Another participant said that her grieving process has made her much kinder towards other people. One told of how her life fell apart when her husband left her, but six years on she is so grateful because she is living a life she could never have imagined. Yet another said, 'I am a natural carer, and the loss and grief I have experience has taught me to stop looking after everyone else. I am *not* responsible for them.'

Many people who come to the Death Cafés say that caring for the dying has helped them to face their own mortality. Others, who talk about sitting at the bedside of a dying relative or friend, often experience a profound spiritual opening for the first time in their lives.

Although it cannot be rushed, the grieving process gives us the opportunity to work through our unresolved losses from the past. I have worked with many clients who came to address a loss they were currently experiencing only to connect suddenly with a grief that they had been sitting on for years. One example is a fifty-year-old female client who was grieving the death of her elderly mother. As she spoke about her feelings, she suddenly realised the confusing intensity of the grief, guilt, fear and anger that she was experiencing was linked to the death of her sister who had drowned at the aged of ten. The shock of her sister's death had a profound impact on her parents' relationship. Both shut down emotionally and grew apart leaving my client, aged eight at the time, alone with the pain and fear that she was facing. Life became a very frightening place for her and, since there had been no closure with what had happened to her sister, my client had developed a terror of death.

Grieving is not about forgetting

Grieving is not about forgetting. It is about being brave enough to open up to the pain and allowing ourselves to cry and sob and wail and howl until the pain eases and grief starts to walk beside us as a life companion rather than a foe.

This is how Marie has come to terms with the death her beloved grandmother and what it taught her. She is now in her early sixties.

I found my grandmother dead on Christmas day. I was twelve at the time. It was a terrible experience. For years afterwards I used to wake up on Christmas morning expecting a dead body rather than a stocking. But I managed to hide away from my grief until my ex-husband, and father of my daughter, died. Even though we hadn't been together for years, I still loved him and, when he went, I felt a part of me died too. His death forced to me confront all the grief I had been holding onto and that made me face my mortality. In fact, I remember suddenly looking at a row of photographs of family members and realising every one of them had died. That's when I understood how out of control we are of when death is going happen. It's made me determined to be as ready as possible. The only thing I want is to see my grandson being born. It's like waiting for spring to arrive. Nature makes me believe that life continues somehow after we are gone – some part of us becomes a visitor somewhere else. I look around at life these days and think, if this is all there is, it doesn't make sense.

I love how Marie reminds us that life is irrepressible, and how all of us are just passing through this physical existence. Grief and loss are an intrinsic part of this physical journey and will continue to teach those to whom we pass on the baton of human experience.

When we don't engage with the profundity of grief and loss it makes us fearful of the future and disconnects us from the life we have. It also makes us angry.

Anger and rage

It's important to understand that anger is a valid, healthy emotion, which enables us to stand up for ourselves and fight our corner. Anger is also a natural part of childhood development. We need to express how we are feeling to make sense of it, and, above all, we need to be heard. However, most of us learn from an early age, particularly in Western cultures, that anger is dangerous and destructive. Therefore, we grow up hiding or repressing what we are feeling. This turns into bitterness, frustration and resentment that we carry into adulthood and project onto others.

There are two types of anger: healthy anger and historic or repressed anger.

Healthy anger is expressed in the moment. It enables us firmly to say 'No' when we know something isn't good for us, to set boundaries, stand our ground, create change for the better and develop self-respect.

Historic or repressed anger is unresolved anger. This may be triggered by something that happens in the present, but it comes steaming out of the past and is expressed as extreme irritation, yelling, exploding, overacting, or violence and abuse.

Unresolved anger

I know how destructive unresolved anger can be. Even though my parents were kind and loving, I was brought up to believe that it was wrong to express anger or to admit to being angry. Our family tradition was to sweep anything unpleasant under the carpet. I had no idea what to do with my anger or frustration so I sulked whenever I felt upset and no one could work out why I developed boils on my stomach and under my arm. This repression turned into chronic depression. My depression led to me to make poor relationship choices because I wanted someone to save me from myself. Of course, no one could, which fuelled my sense of anger and rage at the world.

As I learnt myself, when we do not develop a healthy relationship with anger, we become frightened by it. This stifles our ability to say what we want to say or how to communicate clearly and effectively. Many participants who come to my workshops speak about their impotence around expressing anger and the extreme fear this brings up. One male participant said, 'I don't know how to say what I want to say to my mother. She makes me feel as if I am going insane. I want to shout at her to shut up, but I am too terrified of what that will do.'

Another one admitted, 'I am afraid that if I did admit to my anger, I would be capable of murder. I can't think like that.' Someone else said, 'I feel irritated all the time. I don't know why, but I snap at my husband even though he hasn't done anything. I don't seem to be able to stop myself and I hate myself for it.'

Fear of anger

Fear of anger also makes us drum out anything that anyone else is saying in case we hear what we don't want to. This turns us into over-talkers terrified of silences (although it's interesting how many poor listeners believe they are good listeners) and cuts us off from connecting to the natural world. It also affects our health. For example, repressed anger gives us headaches, backaches, stiff necks, high blood pressure, stomach ulcers, colitis, heart ailments, cancer, boils and skin rashes. Or we develop emotional symptoms such as panic, fear and doubt, depression, addictive behaviours, suicidal tendencies and antidepressant dependency. Or we express our repressed anger towards other people through vindictiveness, blame, bitterness, negativity, joy robbing, criticism, inability to celebrate other's success, violence and abuse.

This may sound a bit extreme, but this is how unexpressed anger plays out in every facet of our society. Nevertheless, I now have hope that anger can help to save our planet. People are being galvanised into action by love *and* anger of how little is being done politically around the world to address serious climate issues. We will return to this in the final chapter.

Rage

Rage is anger rampaging out of control. Rage takes two forms: imploding or exploding. Imploders are immobilised by fear and low self-worth until they finally explode. An example is the distressing account of 64 year-old Sally Challen who beat her husband to death with a hammer after experiencing years of emotional abuse[17]. She was sentenced to life imprisonment for murder but following an appeal this was overturned in 2018 and she was set free on the grounds of diminished responsibility. She speaks with great eloquence about the torment she experienced – and how she finally succumbed to extreme violence – in the hope that it will help others to recognise what emotional abuse can do.

Exploders are those who move rapidly from anger to irrational out of control rage, known as white rage. To feel better about themselves, exploders use white rage to control, terrorise, manipulate and humiliate those around them. Alarming levels of domestic abuse are on the increase. The UK's Office for National Statistics in 2017 estimated that 2.0 million adults, aged between

16 and 59, experienced domestic abuse (1.3 million women, 695,000 men). This has a devastating impact on society because it creates an undertone of trauma, fear and suspicion, which feeds on itself.

Social media is a hotbed of unprocessed rage where people lash out at anyone and anything that triggers a reaction. This is fuelling a blame culture that doesn't know how to take responsibility for what it's creating.

If you are struggling to control your anger or rage, or find yourself addicted to social media trolling or bullying, or if you are living with someone who makes you afraid, humiliated or terrorised, I urge you to seek support and help through counselling, anger management courses, or through your GP. Citizens Advice[18] can also provide information and help.

The way forward

I find it helpful to know that anger is often a secondary feeling, triggered by the primary emotion of being hurt. Therefore, we use anger to protect and defend ourselves from feeling vulnerable and exposed. One way we soothe or hide our pain is through addictive behaviour. Although addictions may provide some form of solace in the short term, they quickly begin to diminish our lives and turn low self-worth into self-hate.

When we learn to acknowledge that our anger is sitting on deep hurt often stemming from childhood traumas, I believe we can begin to find a way to own it and manage it. Managing anger and rage is vital for spiritual wellbeing. I can only repeat that life isn't an easy journey, so the more we take responsibility for what triggers our anger or rage the more we can understand why we behave we way we do.

Breaking addictions

Professor Ruth Engs, from Indiana University, defines addictive behaviour and the addictive process as:

> Any activity, substance, object, or behaviour that has become the major focus of a person's life to the exclusion of other activities, or that has begun to harm the individual or others physically, mentally, or socially is considered an addictive behaviour[19].

In other words, addictions are desire disorders that have become compulsive behaviours. Although addictions may ease our pain for a while, they cannot provide us with the love and connection that we crave. Therefore, as the highs wear off, we start to take more substances to numb the pain or look for other ways to fill the hole inside us. This could be through drink, drugs, smoking, gambling, over exercise, sex, pornography, mobile phones, Internet/texting/twittering, computer games, dating sites, compulsive cleaning and any extreme activity that continually pushes our adrenaline to the limit. It can also be an addiction to food, or not eating, or taking stimulants such as sugar, caffeine, chocolate, and nicotine.

Another way is to adopt bravado and sneer at just about anything and anyone to feel better about ourselves. For example, we turn into know-it-alls – perfectionists, workaholics, dropouts, radicals – in fact, any role that makes us feel superior and different from everyone else. We KNOW we are right, and they are WRONG.

And, then there are those of us who are addicted to emotional drama and suffering. I can certainly identify with that.

Addictive language

Addictive behaviour has a certain language. It goes along the lines of, 'I can give up any time.' 'I only do it because I'm bored.' 'This time I KNOW he's the one.' 'I'm going to give up tomorrow – honestly.' 'I need my mobile phone on all the time because of work.' 'I have to go to the gym twice a day to feel fit.' 'I need six sugars in my tea to get me going in the morning.' 'I know she's angry with me all the time, but I need her.' '*This* diet will work.' 'I must have this pair of shoes.' 'I need to check this out on the Internet right *now*.' 'There's nothing wrong with me, it's you who's got the problem.'

Our addictive behaviours turn our life into the threat and dread of being found out. But our refusal (denial) to face up to what we are doing to ourselves forces us to find more and more ways to engage with our addictions; it creates a vicious cycle that is wrapped up in shame:

After a while our addictions take such a hold on us that we forget how and why they started in the first place. But all the time we know we are destroying ourselves, our relationships and friendships.

Breaking out of the addiction cycle

As I know myself, it takes courage and tenacity of spirit to dig down deep to the source of our hurt so we can break our addictive patterns. We have to develop resilience and self-forgiveness so that along our path to recovery, when we fall down those dark holes, which we all do, we have the inner resources to climb out again. The thing is to keep going and keep forgiving ourselves. We have to keep connected with what it means to be just passing through this human life and understand that we are here to learn and grow.

As I pointed out before, we may feel isolated and alone in our addictions, but actually, we're not. The vast majority of human beings face profound personal and spiritual challenges through some form of addictive behaviour. Confronting our addictions is about developing compassion for ourselves and others. This means taking our addictive behaviour by the hand and saying, 'that's enough now!' And, allowing our thirst for spiritual wellbeing to start gently leading the way.

Many organisations such as Alcoholics Anonymous are built on ever-evolving compassion, love and spiritual wellbeing. They have been set up by recovering addicts to support other addicts to go out into the world, when they are ready, to help yet more addicts. This, to me, is the human condition working at its best. It also makes the statement to me that all of us hold a desire to heal and become whole so we can die at peace.

I spoke to Dr Viv Lucas about how the dying process can be a profound healing process. Viv worked for 23 years as medical director for a Hertfordshire hospice and was president of the palliative care section of the Royal Society of Medicine from October 2017 October 2019. He currently works as a locum palliative care consultant.

I see emotional intelligence as having the ability to identify and respond to our own feelings and the feelings of others. I think that many people die as they have lived. Even though a person cannot be cured, they can still die healed, so I look at my work as healing rather than curing. The word healing means making 'whole.' I see our task as that.

Palliative care is about facilitating the best end to a person's life. We ask them what they want and if they need to do anything to feel more complete. So, it's about helping them to make a better story and to live until they die. For example, they may come in to the hospice in pain, or there's conflict in the family or they may be really angry about something. They may also be afraid of being alone.

It's about working through these issues with them and helping with symptom control. Dame Cicely Saunders, the founder of the modern hospice movement, said it's difficult for those approaching the end of life to attend to other issues when they are overwhelmed by pain or discomfort. I also think it's essential to remember that death and dying is not a medical issue. It's a social condition that's going to happen to us all. There is a danger of over medicalising death, which can stop people from engaging with what's happening to them. I think it's sad that healing has been lost from modern medicine, and most doctors shy away from it because it has connotations, which don't fit into what we regard as professional medical care.

I have had cancer myself, which was successfully treated. I have also experienced the death of my sister from motor neurone disease, my father from old age, and my mother from lymphoma. Their deaths remind me of my own mortality. One day, death is going to happen to me as well.

I think these personal experiences help me to have insights into how patients may be feeling. I have seen some people in a lot of pain. But it's not just physical pain, it's emotional or spiritual pain (what we call 'total pain') when it may be helpful for them to talk about what's going on. I have seen people come into the hospice in considerable pain, which then settles down quite quickly. They know they have entered a place of healing and may have left an environment that isn't conducive to this kind of healing. So, the environment is really important for our well-being. In fact, I see the healing environment as essential. It's all about accepting how things are and emotionally holding people as they die.

I want to die feeling I have lived my life well. We all make mistakes, and I know I am as flawed as anyone else. And, sometimes I have to accept that what I do may not be brilliant, but it is good enough. It makes me appreciate every day and helps me to stop worrying about trivial things, but of course, I still do.

I don't want to be surrounded by medical paraphernalia; I want to end my life in a comfortable environment. Time is only a linear measurement. It doesn't take into account the depth and breadth of someone's life. But I would like my family around. It is really important to tell people how much you love them. Yes, that can be painful, but we need to say our goodbyes. I hope I stay lucid until the end so I can say what I need to say. We could all do a lot more to care for each other. Caring for each other makes us value life and this affects how we relate to nature. We need to care a lot more for nature, too.

I would certainly be relieved to have someone like Viv tending to me during my dying process. Yet, healing is not just about understanding how our emotions and feelings work. The next chapter looks at how our core beliefs and thoughts profoundly affect the way we relate to the world and how we die.

CHAPTER 5

CHANGING CORE BELIEFS

Neuroscience has not yet reached an agreement that thought is energy; however, it does agree that thought *is* potent, and energy follows thought.

Our thoughts form our own inner world created by our experiences, observations and perceptions. This private world is triggered by external stimuli, which interpret what our five senses are experiencing – the sight of a bird, a musical melody, recognising a face in a crowd, going on a first date, kayaking down a river – into a positive, negative or neutral narrative. We either allow what comes into our mind simply to float through our consciousness and disappear or we become caught up in it.

Bruce Lipton, author of *The Biology of Belief* says our conscious mind is thinking 95% of the day, but we are only in control of 5% of it. Many of us go through life believing we are unable to control what's racing through our head, but this isn't so. Across the globe, extensive research into cognitive processing confirms how we all have the ability not just to tame our thoughts, but also to change them. We just need to become conscious of what we are feeling and thinking in the moment, and the sensations these thoughts are creating in our body.

The mind is everything

'The mind is everything,' said Buddha back in 600 BCE. 'What you think you become. If a man speaks or acts with an evil thought, pain follows him. If a man speaks or acts with a pure thought, happiness follows him, like a shadow that never leaves him.'

Ancient scriptures and texts also speak about how our thoughts shape our life. Proverbs 23:7 states, 'For as he thinks in his heart, so he is he.' The Bhagavad Gita, a Hindu holy text written between the fifth and second century BCE, teaches, 'We behold what we are, and we are what we behold.'

There is a plethora of wise and prudent sayings to be found about the power of thought. These are my three personal favourites. The first comes from Plutarch, the ancient Greek philosopher from Delphi who died in 120 AD, who said, 'The mind is not a vessel to be filled, but a fire to be kindled.'

The second quote is from William James, the ninetieth century American philosopher and psychologist. 'The greatest revolution in our generation is the discovery that human beings, by changing the inner attitudes of their minds, can change the outer aspects of their lives.'

The third quote, which makes me laugh every time I read it, comes from Thomas Edison, inventor of the light bulb, who said, 'Five percent of the people think; ten percent of the people think they think; and the other eighty-five percent would rather die than think.'

Tackling negative thoughts

In order to change our lives for the better, we need to understand that we all have core beliefs or thoughts that unconsciously run our lives. A core belief is something that we accept without question. It's as true today as it was yesterday and will be tomorrow. In other words, a core belief is a thought turned into cement.

Our core beliefs either enhance our life or impair it. The table below provides examples of both negative and positive beliefs.

Negative beliefs	Positive believe
I am bad	I am a good person
I am broken	I am whole

I am evil	I am pure light
I am unworthy	I am worthy
I am unlovable	I am loveable
I am fatally flawed (this was my negative core belief for a long time)	I am reaching my full potential
I don't matter	I am open to receive
I hate myself	I love and respect myself
I am dirty	I am free
I am a fraud	I am true to myself

I have left a box for you to write down any negative core belief that may have surfaced as you read through this list, and to identify a positive belief. In my experience, positive and negative beliefs are the opposite sides of the same coin. Writing them as pairs helps us to see the bigger picture of how core beliefs work, and what we would prefer to believe about ourselves.

Positive core beliefs infuse our life with light and enable us to come into alignment with our authentic self. Negative core beliefs steal away our fire and trap us into feelings of shame and low self-worth. They are also insidious. It doesn't take a lot for low self-worth to surface and bop us in the eye. In fact, just about anything good that comes knocking at our door will bring up fear along the lines of, 'I don't deserve this 'or 'I am unworthy.'

Non-deserving means we become resentfully stuck in caring for everyone else yet feel guilty about having needs of our own. Or we are great at telling other people what they should or shouldn't do even though our own life is a mess. Or we stay in relationships that are abusive or devoid of love. Or we have the mind-set that everyone else deserves the very best but not us.

So, how do we change core beliefs that stop us from living fully?

The principles of core beliefs

Our consciousness always aligns with our core belief.[20] This means that if our core belief is positive, we manifest positive experiences. If our core belief is negative, we will manifest negative experiences in our life.

The key to positive manifestation is learning to discipline our mind and focus on changing what doesn't work with clear intent. Until we can do this, we can only manifest at random. Our feral thoughts and desires shoot off all over the place, but we are never in control of what happens to us. We may feel a rush of excitement as something we crave manifests in the moment, but this may not be for our highest good or it doesn't stick around for long. Therefore, when things 'go wrong' or disappear as quickly as they have appeared, it feeds into our negative core beliefs. It's as if we are victims to life, strapped onto a stomach-churning fairground ride that we can't get off. This is not great for developing spiritual wellbeing.

In addition, endlessly repeating positive affirmations without addressing our negative core beliefs may soothe in the short term, but for real change to take place we have to become vigilant and willing to take responsibility for everything that happens to us. Otherwise, as soon as life hurls a curve ball at us (which it will), we find ourselves back in a dark hole that has only been thinly covered over by these positive affirmations. That's when we lose faith and believe the world is plotting against us. These are thoughts and beliefs that we really don't want to take to our deathbed.

Three Equations

I draw three mathematic equations to explain how the theory of core beliefs works to those who come to my workshops and retreats. Seeing them written as mathematical equations seems to help people to understand the principles, so I hope the following will help you, too.

The first equation explains the basic principle of manifestation. I call the second equation the principle of alignment, and the third equation the principle of non-alignment.

Principle of Manifestation
Conscious mind
Conscious Desire + Intent + focus = Manifestation

Unconscious mind
Core Belief

Manifestation works by consciously having a desire and fuelling this desire with intention and focus to bring it about in the physical world. Our desire, intent and focus always align with our core belief.

Principle of Alignment
When we are in alignment with our highest purpose and a positive core belief, the equation looks something like this (I have used abundance as an example).

Conscious mind
(Desire) Abundance +
(Intention) I work creatively +
(Focus) being in service to the
greater good in some way

_____ = Things flow

Unconscious mind
Core belief: I am worthy

Things flow because we are unattached to the outcome, and we trust that the outcome will be for our highest good and the highest good of those around us. We also understand that whatever manifests

– for instance, a person, a situation, an opportunity, or a book that holds exactly the information we are looking for – is often a stepping stone to something else that brings us even more abundance. We are open and receptive to our path unfolding in precisely the right way and at the right time, and we understand that abundance is not just about monetary gain (although it may well be a big part of it): it is about connecting to what gives our life meaning and purpose so we can die feeling complete. The key is that we feel worthy of attracting everything we can possibly need to make our life abundant. And, we are also aware that the world works in mysterious ways. Sometimes not getting what we 'want' may turn into the greatest gift we can imagine.

Principle of Misalignment
When we come from a place of fear, lack and the desire to control the outcome, the equation looks something like this:

Conscious mind
(Desire) I yearn for success +
(Intention) I obsess about money +
(Focus) I fear failure

_____ = **Never enough**

Unconscious mind
Core belief: I am not good enough/
I am unworthy

While our life story is run by unworthy/not good enough core beliefs, we doubt everything. We are hooked into a fear of failure and lack, which feeds our sense of low self-worth. The cycle continues until we do something to address our low self-worth. This is why immensely rich or highly successful people, who appear to have everything that anyone could possibly want, struggle with depression or end up as addicts or kill themselves. No matter who we are or what our status in life may be, we can only feel whole when we shift our negative core beliefs into life-affirming ones.

Changing core beliefs

To change our negative core beliefs, we have to become vigilant. The trick is to catch hold of the negative belief as it pops into our head or shoots up as a physical sensation in our body and defuse it energetically. I can only repeat: awareness is the first step towards making this change. The second step is having the courage to do what it takes to change the way we feel about ourselves. The third step is doggedly committing to change, come what may.

This important inner work profoundly impacts everyone around us. The more we are able to love and accept ourselves, the more we are able to share this love with our family, our friends and the world at large. It also means that as death approaches, we are much more able to allow love to lead us across the threshold.

I interviewed fifty-seven-year old Harriet, who has a successful career in the education sector, about how her 'I'm not good enough' core belief was destroying her life. Her marriage broke down several years ago. Since then she has been desperately searching for a partner, mostly through Internet dating sites:

I became obsessed with finding someone to share my life with, especially as I was approaching sixty. I met a very nice man and dated him for a while, but even though I felt loved by him I thought he wasn't exciting enough. So, I ended the relationship and continued to look for someone better. After several abortive dates I began to feel that maybe I was missing something. That led to a profound insight that nothing was ever good enough for me and this had blighted my life since I could remember. I then realised it was me who never felt good enough. I am now working on changing this belief into 'I have everything I need right now.' This has helped to create more space inside myself to deal with painful childhood issues that created the 'I wasn't good enough' belief. It has been quite a journey of self-discovery. I am more able to deal with all the disappointments I have experienced, which I can now see that I unconsciously created for myself. I find this liberating.

Rocket Man, which portrays Elton John's story, is one of the most powerful films I have seen about the emptiness of fame built on negative core beliefs. The impact that childhood neglect had on Elton John's self-esteem is heart rendering to witness, and I salute his courage and desire to inspire us all to find a way through the pain and suffering that low self-worth causes, and to show us there is a way out.

Once we realise we are co-creators of our reality, we can regain control of what manifests in our life and who and what we attract to ourselves. We also begin to see the journey of life for what it is. An extraordinary diverse adventure filled with experiences from the moment we are born to the moment we die. That's all life is really: a succession of experiences. It's how we respond to them that matters.

I am not saying this is as simple as it sounds. It's taken me years to transform some of my more entrenched negative core beliefs. Yet, each time I change one into a positive belief that really serves my life, I feel more alive and more aligned to the mystery and magic of what life and death has to offer.

After 46 years Liz Christie retired as a psychiatrist and GP in early 2019. She also worked as a psychotherapist and healer. She spoke to me about the importance of maturing psychologically so we can take responsibility for ourselves in a culture that she believes is steeped in the denial of mortality.

Death is the only certainty in life, and I find it hard to understand why people cannot accept this truth. People who refuse to accept they are going to die haven't done the inner work that is needed to find out who they are.

I see this denial as a deep fear of abandonment that surfaces when we are confronted by death. We will do just about anything not to feel abandoned, so we hand ourselves over to others to make the decisions about what happens to us. It's a kind of emotional immaturity or infantilised place that's not spoken about.

I often saw how this played out in collusive relationships between patients who were diagnosed with cancer and oncology specialists. It used to make me incredibly angry. Patients were so terrified of being abandoned by the medical profession they would blindly agree to just any treatment to be 'cured.' But some of these treatments offered nothing more than false hope and had horrendous side effects – sometimes resulting in death directly attributable to the treatment.

I used to say to patients, 'take responsibility for your treatment. Ask what this treatment will do to you. Ask what having chemotherapy really means. Ask about the percentage of people who are cured or die when they agree to a treatment. Ask what your prognosis is.' One of my patients did ask these questions and was told that her prognosis would only increase from 76% to 80%. This helped her to make different choices about her treatment that were far more positive.

Sadly, I believe a lot of the time, we recommend treatments because of who we are as professional doctors, and it's not about the patients. By this I mean we prescribe treatments through fear of litigation, anxiety that we need to be seen to 'do' something, and our own fear of death.

I believe it's time to break through this established patriarchal way of doing things and get away from the belief we can live forever. We can't. Yes, of course, all of us have a deep fear of emotional pain, and this has to recognised and helped sensitively but the truth is that we are only a tiny fleck; a minute flash in the Universe. Everything in nature eventually dies. We are no different. When we talk and share our feelings about death and dying, we begin to normalise it. This requires courage.

Having said all this, I feel conflicted. I confess I don't want to die! I want to live forever. I love life and I want to see my grandchildren grow up. But I know this isn't possible. To help me come to terms with my death, I think about it most days. I want to learn to graciously accept the inevitable and deal with the feelings and thoughts that come up. My biggest fear is not being held through the process of dying. But I have a very supportive family so I know I will be okay. I spend a lot of my time these days reflecting on all the wonderful things in my life. I've learnt it's the little things that really matter. Those sublime moments when you think, 'this is so perfect, I could die right now.' I am also comforted by knowing I have loved, and I have been loved in my life. That's what life and death are all about. Love.

The following chapter takes a deeper look at how trauma and posttraumatic stress disorder (PTSD) makes us question our very existence.

CHAPTER 6

THE INVISIBLE WOUND

~

'Trauma is hell on Earth. Trauma resolved is a gift from the gods,' says American clinical psychologist Peter A. Levine, author of *Waking the Tiger: healing trauma.*

Although it is rarely spoken about, many of us experience suicide ideation or thoughts of suicide when we hit dark times. Behind this is usually a desire for the situation to die rather than actually dying ourselves. These feelings of desperation fade as our life comes back into balance.

However, we can't ignore the impact that unresolved trauma has on our life and how we view death. Trauma rips the rug right out from under our feet. It throws us into turmoil and steals away any sense of joy, making us question our very existence: 'Why has this happened to me?' 'What have I done

107

to deserve this?' 'Why has God picked on me?' 'Why have I been abandoned?'

What is trauma?

The word trauma comes from Greek, meaning 'a piercing or a wounding of a person's psyche.' The good news is that trauma is *not* a fatal disease. With the right care, attention and treatment, it can be healed just like a broken bone.

Trauma has been part of the human condition since we walked out of caves and has been recorded in literature from Homer's *Iliad* and the Old and New Testaments, to Shakespeare's tragedies, and the horrific experiences of the English poets of World War One.

The science of trauma is more recent. It developed through the two World Wars to the diagnosis of PTSD in 1980 when so many traumatised Vietnam Veterans were incapable of returning to 'normal' life when they eventually came home.

The invisible wound

The issue with trauma is the fact that it is an invisible wound. Many people are being medicated for distressing symptoms and behavioural issues rather than receiving treatment for the root cause. This means that people are often carrying around undiagnosed trauma, which has a devastating impact. It makes us feel isolated, lonely, angry, out of control and robbed of the ability to feel and give love. The Centre of Suicide Prevention, based in Canada, states that trauma places us at a higher risk for mental health issues such as depression and addiction, and people who have experienced trauma are at a greater risk of suicide.

How and why we react to trauma depends on what has happened to us in the past. Studies show that those of us who have been deeply traumatised during childhood, particularly through sexual abuse and neglect, are less able to deal with traumatic events during adulthood than children who come from stable homes. Childhood trauma rewires the brain to see the world as terrifying and traps us in the awfulness of what happened.

Undiagnosed trauma is rife in our society. A recent study published by *The Lancet Psychiatry* says that even though most do not develop posttraumatic stress disorder (PTSD), as many as 40% of children and adolescents in the UK and Wales will experience at least one traumatic event in their lifetime. The study states that one in thirteen of these young people go on to develop PTSD, yet many are not receiving the support they need. This means that we are unwittingly creating a section of society, which is overtly fearful and misunderstood. Only recently I heard a tragic story about a teenage girl who had tried to kill herself in a school toilet. She was desperate for help, but neither their parents nor the school were able provide the emotional support she needed. The teenager ended up being sectioned. Her story illustrates the massive impact that trauma has on mental health.

The Limbic System

To understand how trauma affects us physiologically and psychologically, I think it's important to have a brief overview of how our brain is neurologically programmed instinctively and unconsciously to keep us alive. Survival, after all, is a primal instinct, which has allowed us to thrive since before the Stone Age.

Our primal instinct involves the limbic system, the most ancient or reptilian part of ourselves buried deep within our brain, which is responsible for our fight, flight, freeze survival mechanism.

Our limbic system consists of the Amygdala and the Hippocampus.

1. Amygdala (functions from birth).
Perceives threat. Alarms the hypothalamus, which activates survival hormones. Restores our body to equilibrium after threat of trauma has passed.
2. Hippocampus (develops between our second and third year).
Processes data to make sense of what has happened autobiographically. Delivers information to (left) pre-frontal cortex (or area of logical thinking). Gives us

the ability to recount what happened in chronological order.

In the meantime ...

In the meantime, threat signals are being sent to the prefrontal cortex, home of rational thinking. This journey takes 250 milliseconds, or three times as long. Therefore, it's important to understand that we have no control over our instinctual fight, flight or freeze reactions. They are completely automatic and unconscious responses to the perceived or actual threat.

It's only after the danger has passed that we can rationalise what has happened. This can add to the distress. For example, victims of attack or rape who freeze in the moment will often find it difficult to come to terms with why they didn't fight back. When they understand they had no conscious choice in the way they instinctively reacted in order to survive, it helps them to release shame and guilt.

How our brain perceives a threat

We no longer live in a time when we need a pump of adrenaline to fight off an attack from a sabre-toothed tiger. But our survival instincts are just as potent in modern life. Adrenaline is triggered by anything that we *perceive* as a threat, including trying to survive in a highly aggressive, competitive and death denying society. How we deal with these perceived threats depends on our emotional make-up.

For example, when we have developed a strong sense of self and inner connection, we are more curious and at ease with what life presents us. We can see the bigger picture and make informed choices about the life we would prefer to live. However, when we are carrying unresolved trauma, we experience the world as hostile and menacing. This ramps up our levels of adrenaline and puts us on hyper-alert twenty-four hours a day.

Two types of trauma

There are two types of trauma: Big Ts and small ts.

Big Traumas or 'Big Ts' are sudden, massive experiences. These can be human created such as accidents, violence, rape, murder, traumatic childbirth, sudden death, abortion, war, knifings, shootings or muggings. Other examples are natural disasters such as earthquakes, tsunamis, volcanoes, tornadoes and hurricanes. People are more able to recover from natural disasters than human created traumas. This is because natural disasters are usually regarded as 'an act of God,' whereas human-created traumas trigger our abhorrence, horror or despair about the darker side of human nature. However, every continent on Earth is now affected by climate change, in some part induced by our disregard for the planet. Right at this moment, Sheffield, in the north of England, is under several feet of flood water and ferocious fires are eating up vast areas of California in the US and in Queensland, Australia. This is having an impact on how we view natural disasters.

Small Traumas or 'little ts' are long term and insidious experiences such as bullying, harassment, chronic disease, famine, child abuse, violence in the home, divorce, poverty, social deprivation, political torture, refugee status, and repeated exposure to trauma as front line responders. People can be exposed to these little 'ts' for a long time until one day something explodes. The person ceases to function, or they go on the attack. Many school shootings, for example, are carried out by those who have been systematically bullied or abused, or who have been shunned by their community.

Traumatic events

Big traumas can be experienced in three ways:

1. Through direct personal experience involving actual or threatened death or serious injury, or other threat to a person's physical integrity.
2. Witnessing an event involving actual or threatening death or serious injury, or other threat to a person's physical integrity.

3. Learning about unexpected or violent death, or serious harm, or threat of death or injury experienced by a family member or close associates.

During a traumatic event, the person often experiences helplessness, hopelessness and horror, and believes they are about to die. PTSD develops when, for a variety of reasons, our mind finds it difficult to process what has happened to us, with the result that traumatic feelings, thoughts, images and sensations get 'stuck' in the neurological pathways of our brain. Our body continues to release adrenaline as if the threat is still present, causing continued, long-term distress.

There are three main indicators that someone has developed PTSD.

1. We may continually experience intrusive memories or dreams (Intrusion).
2. We may numb out in some way to the distressing and painful memories of what happened (Avoidance/numbing).
3. Our adrenaline levels have not returned to normal, so we believe we are still under attack (Hyperarousal).

Trauma symptoms

A person with PTSD might not have to all of these symptoms but may experience several.

INTRUSION	AVOIDANCE/ NUMBING	HYPERA-ROUSAL
• Intrusive recollections (images, sounds, even smells) • Dreams/ nightmares • Distress when exposed to reminders • Flashbacks	• Avoidance of related thoughts/ feelings • Avoidance of reminders such as places, streets, certain people • Emotional distancing from others • Inability to feel pleasure • Sense of no future • Losing the sense of self • Forgetting	• Irritability/ angry outbursts • Sleeping difficulties • Poor concentration • Hyper vigilance • Exaggerated startle (e.g. car backfire) • Panic attacks • Physical symptoms – sweats / aches / migraines

Human beings are incredibly resilient and, even though it may feel very uncomfortable for a few weeks, most who are exposed to a Big T traumatic event will not go on to develop PTSD. With social support and recognition of what they've been through, people usually begin to feel better within a couple of months. However, as I know from my own personal experience of trauma and working as a psychotherapist specialising in trauma, recovery depends on the person's outlook, past unresolved traumas, childhood experiences, perception of whether their life remains at risk, and continuous exposure to traumatic events.

Healing trauma

Trauma fragments our memory of what's happened to protect us from the worst part of the event. This is why many people often find it incredibly hard to piece together their traumatic experience so they can make sense of it. To heal we need to recreate a coherent story of what happened, including the missing parts. Extensive post-traumatic research suggests that between 30% and 70% of people who experience trauma report a positive change and growth as they begin to recover[21]. There is a shift in their perception as they turn what happened into a cohesive story. This helps them to create distance from 'being a victim' to someone who can begin objectively to make sense of it all.

116

Creating a narrative

Creating a cohesive story of our life also plays an essential part in the way we die. In the BBC2 Horizon documentary, *We Need to Talk about Death*,[22] consultant anesthetist and presenter Dr Kevin Fong, points out the importance of reclaiming the narrative of our life so we can die a better death. I will never forget interviewing a health care worker for an end-of-life experience study that I was researching with Dr Peter Fenwick. She told me about a very angry thirty-year-old man she had looked after. He was raging, she said, and most people didn't want to go near him. But she felt there was something going on that he wasn't expressing. So, she invited him to write down what he was feeling inside. 'He suddenly started writing reams and reams of paper – everything that had happened to him, and what it had done to him, and what he had done to others. This went on for days.' She said it was as if he was writing himself out of his life but making sense of it all as well. Finally, he began to make peace with himself, and eventually he died at peace.

A consultant palliative care consultant told me another extraordinary story of an elderly Jewish woman under his care who became deeply confused and distressed. She was convinced she had been raped in the hospital and insisted on making a formal complaint to the hospital authorities. The palliative team called in her son and told him what was happening. He told them that his mother had witnessed her sisters being attacked by Nazis during the Second World War. She had somehow escaped but had never spoken about the trauma of what happened. The palliative care team brought in the Rabbi to talk to her. The rabbi was with the woman for three days. The consultant had no idea what they spoke about, but her talk with the Rabbi allowed the woman to die in peace.

Both of these end of life carers recognised the importance of helping their patients to make sense of what was going on for them so they could let go of their trauma. To die at peace, we need to make sense of our lives no matter how difficult and painful this may be.

If you identify with any trauma symptoms, try to find help. It's important to educate ourselves about trauma as much as possible. Understanding the impact of trauma helps us to take back control of our life and to understand that we are not dealing with a terminal illness. Trauma is an injury, which can often be treated successfully. The National Institute for Health and Clinical Excellence, a specialist health authority within the NHS, recommends Eye Movement Desensitization and Reprocessing (EMDR)[23] and Trauma-focused Cognitive Behavioural Therapy (CBT) as treatments.

To conclude this chapter, I spoke to Dr John Ryder who is a medical psychotherapist (a psychiatrist with higher training in psychotherapy – in John's case, he is a psychoanalytic psychotherapist) about the effect that trauma has on how we live and die, and the importance of seeking help from someone we trust. He has been working with mental health issues for forty years.

Trauma certainly impacts how we die. Life and death are interlinked so if we have a difficult or traumatic relationship with life, we tend to develop a difficult relationship with death. For example, we might wish to die or we attempt suicide, or we develop a hatred of life. These feelings are complex because inside us all is a deep longing for love, which often drives us to go for the wrong thing. This choice leads to more disappointment and so the cycle continues until we break out of the trauma.

Trauma splits our psyche. This split affects or interrupts our natural experience of what it means to develop as individuals in the world. It figuratively stands in our way. People who are traumatised are constantly terrified of going back to the experience of what has already happened, but this is not experienced as being in the past, but as happening in the present. With the potential for it to be triggered at any moment, they are continually on guard. It is called hypervigilance. This directly affects how we relate to other people. When we carry trauma, we can't be fully present in relationships. We can't be present because we're not whole.

Trauma can successfully be treated, but it does mean developing the courage to open up to those unpleasant memories and feelings, which make us feel most vulnerable.

My work is about helping people to develop a safe refuge within themselves so they can learn to trust another person with their pain. Feeling safe comes through being attended to without impingement. This may be the healing part of the therapeutic encounter, which provides a safe, controlled environment where the person can begin to integrate what happened to them into an episodic story. It also creates a space where all those split off parts caused by the trauma can begin to come back together. Healing is about growing into a whole state of being and togetherness. It becomes possible through developing a secure place of refuge inside: usually through experiencing being loved. People may find a safe place in varied ways. For example, some people develop religious or spiritual faith or find safety with animals, or take refuge in music and the arts, or have a place in nature where they feel soothed.

I suspect that the more open we are and the more we let go of fear, the less problematic death becomes. Perhaps death can be compared to giving birth. Complications aside, the more a woman allows herself to move through labour, rather than resist it, the more she becomes in tune with her body and her baby. There's a sense of natural flow. Death seems like that, too. It's about surrendering to the power that works through nature and allowing this to move us through our dying process.

I want to die in a peaceful setting, somewhere calm with fresh air around so I can release into dying. I think I want to die consciously. I don't mind the thought of dying alone, but it must be lovely to die with someone who is tuned into you in a prayerful state and, at the same time, is not intrusive. I can't really imagine what dying is going to be like. If you choke on something you automatically panic. I don't like the thought of that. But then other things are happening at the same time in the body, so I guess it won't be like that anyway. I imagine dying is the same as deep meditation, when your breath gets finer, until it seems you may never breathe again, as you open up and let go. Who knows? I feel sad to think that I won't be here to witness the beauty of this life anymore, but life is constantly changing anyway. It's all about being fully present.

Engaging in post-traumatic recovery and psychological healing is essential for spiritual wellbeing. In the next chapter we explore how we appear to be called constantly to a deeper understanding of who we are as we travel through life.

CHAPTER 7

SOULQUAKES

As the previous chapters point out, some of us experience far more challenging, traumatic and stressful lives than others. On the other hand, some people genuinely love their life and it appears that although these people encounter upsets, disappointments and distress, they don't experience the depth of suffering that many of us do. I call these 'gift lives.' Then there are those of us whose life trundles by with relatively little happening apart from routine work and family commitments. Even so, boredom or monotony does come with its own challenges.

In whatever way we experience life, it's advisable to remember that everything in the known universe is in a continual state of flux. And so are we. I see our entire life journey as a naturally evolving cycle of endings and beginnings which continue to progress until we draw our final breath. However, we often become so swept up in trying to keep our noses above the water level of life that we forget how endings and beginnings teach us about letting go of the old so we can welcome in the new. Instead, we become stuck between the known and unknown, and start to panic because we don't know how to move forward.

In a sacred context, this space between the known and unknown is about stepping across the threshold into liminal space.

Liminal Space

Liminal comes from the Latin *Limen* meaning Threshold. The concept of liminality was studied by the twentieth-century French anthropologist Arnold van Gennap who witnessed tribal rites and rituals, and the importance of preparing for the transition from one state or stage of life into another. For example, young people ritualistically and consciously preparing for adulthood.

As such, he discovered that native cultures do not believe we live a linear life and then drop off our perch into oblivion. Rather they believe that life is a spiritual evolutionary process, which involves a natural rhythm of activity and progress, followed by periods of withdrawal and preparation for what comes next. Van Gennap realised that native cultures recognised these times of withdrawal as a state of sacred transition into and through the liminal space.

However, anthropologist Victor Turner, whose work draws on Arnold van Gennap's research, says that the liminal space is very hard to come by in the modern and now post-modern world. He considers that we are have become too strategic, functional, and hurried to 'easily seek what the ancients sought above all else [spiritual liberation].' He states that only painful experiences are now strong enough to lead us into 'this unique place where all significant transformation happens.' I find this really disturbing; but I believe he's right. Most of us are so terrified of silence and the 'not-doing' that any form of withdrawal is unthinkable.

I empathise with how leadership facilitator Heather Plett says there is something in our nature and culture (especially in the West) that has conditioned us to want the easy path. She states, "We want to get to 'spiritual' without taking the journey through 'messy'".[24]

Nevertheless, crossing the threshold into liminal space *is* about getting emotionally messy because it presents us with the dark and frightening space of non-action. At some stage in our life, we *will* face an ending that will leave us hanging in mid-air. When we accept that we have entered a sacred liminal space, it gives us time to turn it into spiritual reflection. This means consciously going within to assess what we really need while we wait for the next step in life to show itself. As the Dalai Lama says, 'Silence is often the best answer.'

The Liminal Space

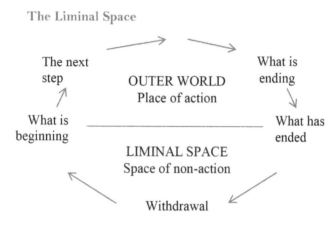

In my workshops I use an exercise to help participants to understand what their liminal space is showing them, which they can either draw or write down. I encourage them to ask questions. For instance, what does this liminal space look like? What does stepping into liminal space feel like? What does it want from you? What do you want from it? What message does it carry for you right now?' This helps them to go beyond the fear, frustration, confusion, and even panic of non-action to accept that when the time is right, things will come clear again in a much more conscious and informed way.

Prying fingers off the edge of the ledge

For those of us who do not readily engage with the ebb and flow of life, it seems that something comes along to pry our fingertips off the edge of the ledge.

It's as if our inner 'Me' conspires with the Universe to shake us out of our comfort zone, often with the biggest firecracker possible. I call this a Soulquake moment.

Soulquakes appear when we are resistant to change or refuse to engage with change even though everything seems to be yelling at us to pay attention. They happen when we are so overloaded with the stuff of life that we have ceased to listen to ourselves or to others. They materialise when we think we are in control or become too complacent with life, or we start to believe that we are invincible, immortal, separate and superior to everyone else.

Soulquakes can manifest as an immediate crisis or a nagging feeling that something 'ain't right' which eventually turns into acute discomfort or stress.

Generational soulquakes

A study by psychologist Dr Oliver Robinson in 2013[25] illustrates how soulquakes (life crisis in his terminology) are also generational. For example, his study showed that people in their thirties often experienced a crisis in their work situation or had relationship break-ups.

For those in their forties, a parent dying often becomes a major issue for women, but for men it is, "Holy crap, I've got a lot to do". I should add that I have increasingly met many women who are also expressing the same 'Holy crap' sentiments as they pass forty, and many are still having babies. The Office for National Statistics stated in 2018 that over-forty mothers are the only age group with a rising conception level in the UK.

Robinson's study reports that women (and men) in their fifties often experience major upheaval due to identity crisis and/or health problems. I include the impact of the menopause here. While researching and writing *Sex, Meaning and the Menopause,* I was shocked at how few women approaching their fifties are prepared for the menopause, how it affects their life, their status at work and their relationship. For many women it marks profound health and psychological changes, a possible dip in libido, and in some cases the end of their marriage. The sharp rise in menopause websites and workshops (including in the workplace) shows how menopausal women (and their husbands and partners) are hungry for information, which will help them to understand what the hell is going on. It's also heartening to know that a number of British MPs are pushing for clear workplace policies to protect women going through the menopause.

For those in their sixties, Robinson reports how crises often centre around retirement-related issues, financial issues, health issues, and a heightened awareness of mortality. His study also identified that one in three people between sixty and sixty-nine will experience a life-altering crisis such as bereavement, breakdown in relationship, or becoming caught up in caring for a family member. This fact is supported by *Research by Carers UK*, which identifies that one in eight adults are carers who are often looking after an elderly relative or parent-in-law.

The sandwich generation

Again, I would add that numerous older people are also experiencing what is now known as *the sandwich effect*. Although grandparents often find it enriching to look after their grandchildren, some find this stressful, especially when caring for elderly relatives as well. I have often heard workshop participants in their sixties say, 'When is it my turn to have some fun?'

'The sixties is the 'new awkward age', says Robinson. 'Until very recently, people who reached their sixties just sat back and enjoyed what time they had left, but that's certainly not what the baby boomers are doing.'

I agree with him. We baby boomers are certainly ageing differently from our parents' generation. We may be the next generation to start dying off but, thanks to modern health practices, we could have many more years ahead of us. Yet, we are swimming in uncharted waters. An extended life span seems to be creating as much emotional turmoil, uncertainty, loneliness and isolation as the desire for freedom and independence that countless baby boomers are now seeking and have come to expect as their right.

This is taking its toll on relationships. The Office for National Statistics cites the largest group of divorcees in the UK as fifty-five onwards. Aptly named the Silver Separations, research conducted by UK's Health Promotion Agency states that we baby boomers are one of the biggest groups to catch sexually transmitted diseases.[26] This could be due to the fact that many older people associate sexual safeguarding with pregnancy protection. As a study by *Saga Magazine* reports, 10% of people over fifty say they are not practising safe sex, but they have no idea that they are putting themselves, or their spouse, at risk. Now, that's a soulquake I can do without.

If you want to make God laugh, tell him your plans

We've established that soulquakes are part of the human condition. They happen beyond our conscious control to shake us up, and we know that life is never going to be the same again.

During the immediate aftermath of a profoundly distressing soulquake that happened to me a few years back, I felt I had been blown off my feet and thrown into the bottom of a deep ravine at the edge of the world. Nonetheless, even though I was profoundly shocked by what happened, I knew deep inside that this was for my highest good and, however painful, in time the experience would enrich who I was.

Although it took several years to climb back out of my ravine, this proved to be true. As I began to open up to life again, out of nowhere, positive and productive opportunities started to come my way and, just like a river finds its course, my new life found its own direction without my trying to push it. I am constantly filled with awe at how life mysteriously and magically works out for the best. So, yes, if you want to make God laugh, tell him your plans.

Finding 'Isness'

My soulquakes have helped to deepen my faith and connection with something far greater than myself. To me this something far greater is the boss – but a boss who thrives on cohesive teamwork. We both know that we have to work closely together for my highest good to blossom. This, for me, means becoming present in the moment and practicing 'Isness.' Life is just what it is.

Isness is not about demolishing our ego (our 'I'-personality) – we need our ego to get out of bed in the morning. It's about educating it and working with it. This doesn't mean becoming passive either. In fact, for me, it's the complete opposite. But I find I am no longer driven by the need for success or recognition to feel good about myself. Yes, I carry the scars of life, but these days I'm okay with who I am and, as long as I stay open to learn and grow, I believe that my spiritual wellbeing can only strengthen.

Success, to me, is being willing to respond to the higher call to help make this world a better place, whether it is writing a book, running a workshop or just smiling at a stranger in the street. The reward is knowing that, in my own small way, I can make a difference.

I particularly like how Father Richard Rohr, Franciscan monk, author and teacher who set up the Centre for Action and Contemplation in the US, regards the role of personal crisis. In one of his daily meditations he states, 'We *must* stumble and fall, I am sorry to say. We must be out of the driver's seat for a while, or we will never learn how to *give up* control to the Real Guide[27].'

The Noble Purpose

One of the most moving books I have read about the power of post-traumatic growth is *Man's Search for Meaning* by Viktor Frankl, an Austrian Jewish neurologist and psychiatrist. Somehow, during his interment in Auschwitz, and other concentration camps, he found the strength, resilience and faith not only to survive but also to use his experiences to help other prisoners make sense of their own trauma and suffering.

Bearing witness to so many violent and tragic deaths, he began to understand how and why some people had the inner resources to cope and survive the appalling atrocities they faced daily. He divided these into three reasons.

1. The hope of being re-united with much loved people again (Frankl talked in his head to his beloved wife every day even though, at the time, he had no idea she was dead).
2. They had projects they were determined to complete.
3. They possessed a great faith.

Frankl realised that there is a driving force within us all to find personal meaning in life – what we are doing here, and why – and that finding meaning is a profoundly individual journey which has to be discovered rather than invented. He considered that crises present a challenge to be overcome, and life is not about gaining pleasure or avoiding pain. Rather, it's about seeking what really matters and finding out what spurs us forward. Frankl said, 'When we can no longer change a situation, we are challenged to change ourselves.'

'Out of suffering have emerged the strongest souls; the most massive characters are seared with scars,' said Kahlil Gibran, Lebanese artist, poet, and author of *The Prophet*. Eckhart Tolle, spiritual teacher and author of *A New Earth,* speaks of suffering as a 'Noble purpose: the evolution of consciousness and the burning up of the ego.' I really love these teachings, and, when things have been bleak, I read them every day.

Suffering shows us who we really are

'I want to be thoroughly used up when I die,' said Irish playwright George Bernard Shaw, 'For the harder I work, the more I live. Life is no 'brief candle' to me. It is a sort of splendid torch which I have got hold of for a moment, and I want to make it burn as brightly as possible before handing it on to the future generations.' Me, too!

My own experience of suffering has been harsh, raw, and intensely soul penetrating. Yet, I couldn't write this book unless I had been through the trauma, pain and loss, which I have experienced. Similar to many people I have spoken to about their recovery from soulquakes, my suffering has reconnected me to the 'Me' I am deep inside. It has also helped me to become much more compassionate when I hear other people talk about their battles with life and their fear of death. So, for me, even though it can be horribly painful, our brokenness, when we allow it, opens the door to spiritual wellbeing and personal transformation.

One of the most inspiring stories I have encountered about personal transformation concerns Dwayne Fields[28]. He was born in Jamaica but was brought up on a council estate in inner city London. He talks candidly about the street gangs and violent crime that influenced his early years. However, following a life-threatening gun incident, he realised he had to do something to get away or he would be sucked into a life he didn't want.

In 2010 Dwayne became the first black Briton to walk to the North Pole (his account of confronting the cold is hilarious). This trip started his passion for championing intercity youngsters to engage with the countryside and become adventurers in their own right. From such underprivileged and potentially violent beginnings, Dwayne has been awarded the Freedom of the City of London and is now a Fellow of the Royal Geographical Society. If he can change his life, any of us can.

Another story, which touches me deeply, is how Eric Clapton overcame horrendous drug addiction and alcoholism. He speaks openly about his difficult and traumatic relationship with his mother and how his painful, early childhood experiences instilled a sense of worthlessness in him. Even though he became one of the greatest guitarists in the world, he was constantly sabotaging himself and his relationships. Clapton was in recovery prior to the tragic death of his four-year old son, but the trauma prompted him to get back to work writing and recording songs. In the immensely moving documentary Life in 12 Bars, he admits that he wanted to make a success of his life for his son to be proud of him. In 1998 he founded The Crossroads Centre, a substance-abuse rehabilitation centre for drug and alcohol addiction located on the Caribbean islands of Antigua and Barbuda. Clapton remarried and now has four daughters. He continues to bring joy to millions of fans worldwide through his music and live performances, and to be a source of inspiration for others going through their journey of recovery.

To my mind, this is what developing spiritual wellbeing is about.

However, Caroline Evans, founder of Essentia for Counselling and Psychotherapy, who has specialised in trauma and relationship therapy for the past seventeen years, says she is continually astonished at how few clients speak about spirituality during their therapy sessions.

> Even though clients will talk about painful and difficult areas, I have never had a client coming to me because they want to talk about their own mortality. I find that fascinating because I believe that if we can't accept the inevitability of death, we can't fully live. I often ask clients to name one thing that is guaranteed in their life. The usual answer is something along the lines of, 'my house.' I see the shock in their eyes when I say, 'Death is our only guarantee.' I had one client who was so in denial that after they had been diagnosed with a terminal illness, they would only refer to it as 'the problem,' and wanted solution focused therapy to overcome it.
>
> Many people I come across are ignorant of what living a full life actually means. To me, it's finding the balance between the physical, emotional, mental and spiritual areas of who we are. People desperately want this, but they may never have considered that they have a spiritual side. It makes me sad because many

clients are terrified of 'getting it wrong', or 'not being good enough' or being 'a failure.' This makes them feel ashamed and unhappy, and they don't have the understanding that this can change.

When I talk about spirituality, there's often almost a sense of bewilderment and even panic because they either associate spirituality with religious belief or someone who sits in a circle and hugs trees. It's quite a big step for them to understand that there is a higher power that can help them to reflect on their life. I start with a very simple exercise, such as inviting them to look out of the window and tell me what they see. They might talk about the grass, or a flower, or a bird flying by. This begins to open the door to an understanding that something else exists beyond their emotional turmoil. I can see clients physically change as they start to connect with themselves and to discover they have an inner voice. It's as if their life force enters their body for the first time.

Working with so many people in denial of death makes me think of my own death. I want to die as well as I possibly can, and without regret. Of course, I will be sad to say goodbye to those I love, but I see my death as a fluid continuation of my life. I look at my life as a whole and, as I grow older and more accepting of my death, I become less attached to material possessions. I like simplifying my life and reflecting on things that aren't 'human.' I look at myself as doing the best I can possibly do with who I am. I can only follow what feels right. Helping people to connect with their spirituality and mortality is something that certainly feels right to me.

I hope Caroline's interview will inspire you to think about how important it is to engage with what spirituality means to you. The next chapter provides practical help to deepen your understanding of spiritual wellbeing and to find ways to connect back to who you are.

CHAPTER 8

HELPING YOURSELF

Becoming happier is about consciously finding ways to release what makes us unhappy. This is not about blaming or criticising anyone else for what's happened to us. Rather, as I keep repeating, it's about learning to take personal responsibility. I describe someone who does this work as a linage breaker. It's a person who has the courage to draw a line under any inherited predispositions or conditioned negative patterns and beliefs and *refusing* to indulge them anymore.

Yes, it can be very painful and frightening to let go of entrenched patterns and beliefs. One spiritual teacher I came across on my own path of recovery explained how our negative beliefs and patterns are like wearing a very old, comfortable jumper. It may be full of holes and fit only for the bin, but it's an effort to take it off and what on earth would we replace it with anyway? But that's just what we need to do. So how do we strip off this useless old jumper? Here are some suggestions:

Talking Therapy

When you are serious about your healing journey, you may want to find a therapist who can support you. Friends and family can be good to talk to, but they usually have their own agendas and often proceed to fix you or talk about what's happening in their own life rather than create an open receptive space where you can explore what's going on.

Many therapists in private practice have a fee structure, so it's always worth enquiring about that. Some local counselling services (depending on where you live) are free or accept donations and staffed by volunteer counsellors. National organisations, such as Cruse Bereavement, offer a number of free sessions that focus only on bereavement issues, which can limit the therapeutic process. Most GP surgeries can arrange for six free counselling sessions with a trained counsellor but seldom offer on-going therapeutic support and there's often a waiting list.

If you choose to go into talking therapy, be mindful of what kind of therapy feels right for you. For example, some therapeutic practices are analytically, cognitively based or solution focused (working with negative thought patterns) while others work with person-centred, existential or transpersonal models (the synergy of the whole person). For those who have experienced profound trauma or childhood abuse, you may need to find specialist help.

Speaking for myself, I am cautious about being tied for years into a therapeutic relationship. As I grew to know myself more, I needed the freedom to explore different issues at different times with different therapists. On the other hand, many people are more drawn to form a long-term relationship with one particular therapist so trust and safety can build over time. Whatever the therapeutic model, I believe it's the relationship you form with your therapist that matters. You need to feel comfortable and safe with them for the 'click' to happen. As I know from my own experience of working as a psychotherapist, when the click happens, the magic begins.

Remember, this is your life, your journey, and ultimately your death. You are in charge of how you want to proceed along your life path, and I would counsel against becoming swayed by anyone (no matter who they are) telling you what is right or wrong for you. You will know, and, if you don't, you will soon find out.

Alternative therapies

Over the past three decades there has been an explosion of alternative therapies such as shamanism, acupuncture, aromatherapy, ayurvedic medicine, reiki, soul retrieval, hypnotherapy, healing gongs, voice work, singing, dancing and yoga.

Apart from acupuncture (although only in limited cases) few, if any, of these are available on the NHS. So, taking the alternative therapy route may become a little pricey. Again, it's a matter of trusting what you are intuitively drawn to do and the teacher or tutor you feel comfortable with. I know of someone who had very little money but knew she needed the on-going help of a particular alternative therapist. She regarded the money she spent as an investment not just in herself, but also in her children's welfare and the relationship with her husband. She told me she was amazed at how the money she needed to pay each week for her healing always turned up – often in the most unexpected ways. She told me, 'It was as if the Universe was cheering me on.'

Mindfulness has now become mainstream. There's lots of information about mindfulness on the Internet, so you can practice mindfulness for free. Similarly, as Paul Wilson talks about at the end of this chapter, you can practice five simple steps to wellbeing for free too. The important thing is to engage with something that sustains you and supports your journey.

Workshops

Workshops are another way to develop spiritual wellbeing. As I mentioned in the introduction, I was so desperate to find out who I was that, for a while, I became a fully signed up workshop junkie.

Workshops can be great fun because we get to meet like-minded people and we can forge really strong relationships. Remember, we are programmed to connect, and it can be such a relief to know that we are not the only one thinking and feeling the way we do, or struggling to make sense of life, or we are scared to accept that one day we're going to die and so is everyone else that we know and love.

Workshops can be emotionally challenging and sometimes life changing. If you feel drawn to a workshop, explore it. It's a good idea to find out about the workshop leader before signing up; it's about trusting your heart. It's also wise to be aware that workshops can induce emotional and psychic highs that tend to send you orbiting into another stratosphere and you may come back to Earth with a bump when you return to 'normal' life afterwards.

Still, as Gregg Braden, author of *The Divine Matrix*, says, there comes a time when you need to 'put aside the workshops and crystals and do it for yourself.' I agree with that. We all have whatever we need inside ourselves. Workshops are there to give us the permission, tools, and context to release our fears and limitations so we can start to believe in who we are. Once we practice self-belief, we can begin to contribute positively to the wellbeing of others who are struggling with the human condition. But, as I have learnt myself, we *have* to do our own inner work first.

Self-help books

There are thousands of excellent personal growth and spiritual development books on the market. There are also an increasing number of books, podcasts and YouTube videos, which speak about the spiritual importance of dying consciously and on death and consciousness. I have included some titles that I have found particularly useful at the end of the book.

However, I would be wary about the get-everything-you-want-quick New Age books that promise you instant enlightenment, total abundance, or anything else you can think of. As we explored in Chapter 6, until we transmute our negative beliefs into positive ones, what we manifest tends to appear and disappear like the mists of Avalon.

Finding your tribe

One of the most sustaining things we can do for ourselves is to find our tribe. This isn't about family or even old friends. This is finding people who really resonate with us and are prepared to help and support our growth and development, which goes both ways.

I speak to many people waking up to a new way of being who are confused by how those they have known for years seem to drop away, or they find it increasingly difficult to resonate with family members. Some say they seem to have no friends left at all, and it makes them feel lonely. Yet this is a natural part of the process of engaging with spiritual wellbeing. When we start to evolve onto a different level of understanding we change energetically, too. We are organically called to seek out people who are also waking up so we can have far more meaningful conversations. Many people also talk about a desire to live communally with like-minded people. Any perceived or longed for utopia will have its pros and cons like anything else, but it's the sense of forming a like-minded community, which is the draw. Others find they want to spend much more time alone, even to withdraw completely from life for a while.

So, this is a good moment to look around at those in your life. Do your close relationships feed and nurture your spiritual growth? Do your friends support your desire to explore the meaning of life? Or are you fruitlessly spending hours listening to their dramas knowing they have no intention of changing things? Do you feel drained by them? Do they actually listen to *you*? Do you feel lonely or invisible when you are with them? Do you feel frustrated and irritated by chit-chat that lacks insight and depth? These are indicators that life is changing for you, and maybe it's time to open up for new people to come into your life.

Welcoming silence

We have created a modern world, which is so terrified of silence that we think it's weird when people want to be in silence. Yet it's through silence that we can begin to create a space inside ourselves so we can come back to ourselves.

We can find silence or quiet by going on silent retreats (which I do regularly), by going to a meditation, yoga or tai chi class or creating quiet time at home or somewhere in nature.

When creating a quiet time, I prefer to use the word 'sitting'. Sitting for me is being relaxed in my favourite chair, connected with the rhythm of my breath, and allowing my thoughts to wander in and out of my head until a moment comes when they just fade away. It may not last for long, but it's a wonderful feeling when it happens. I also follow the advice of Father Richard Rohr, who confesses that static praying or meditating for a long time can be difficult. He promotes prayerful, mindful movement, which also quietens the mind.

This is as simple as going for a walk on your own and allowing the natural world to soothe you. It may involve sitting at the base of a tree enjoying the support of the tree trunk or enjoying a dip in a river, or going for a paddle in the sea or working in the garden.

Silence strengthens the core of who we are, so we become more able to sit quietly with other people without feeling awkward or anxious, or needing to fill the silence with yet more noise. I often think what the world must have sounded like in pre-industrial days. In country settings, noise would have centred on the clop of horse hooves; the hiss of fires; the rustle of leaves; the songs of birds;

the bellow of cattle. If you are someone who can't imagine what it's like to be without noise, or the thought of silence frightens you, or you are scared of being alone with yourself, make a little space by turning off your music and your phone; light a candle to the silence and see what happens when the silence greets you. Initially, you may be able to tolerate it for only a few seconds, but each time you enter into the silence, you may be surprised at how you begin to enjoy and even relish it.

Use your imagination

Imagination is our most powerful self-healing gizmo. I love how French philosopher Joseph Joubert described imagination as 'the eye of the soul.' We all have imagination. If you think you haven't, picture a lemon in your mind's eye. Chop it in half and then lick the flesh. Just writing this makes my salivary glands wince. Some people find creative imagination easy. For some, it takes practice. Others find it difficult to visualise things, but they may hear or sense things instead. Do whatever works for you. The thing is to start using your imagination to help you to feel more at home with who you are.

The following, simple, creative mind exercises will help you to build a feeling of inner safety so you can begin to defuse difficult and painful feelings. They can also help to quieten that vicious little voice in your head which keeps telling you how rubbish you are.

You may need to repeat these exercises many times or find other creative ways to confront what's hijacking your life. As I have said before, awareness is the first step. Dogged determination to change is the second.

When I do powerful inner work, I turn off my phone, find a quiet space and light a candle to myself. This turns what I am doing into a sacred ritual and helps me to connect with my inner 'Me'.

Creating a safe place

Turn off your phone and find a quiet place where you won't be interrupted. Settle into wherever you chose to sit or lie. Take several deep, slow, breaths to relax your body. If you are feeing anxious, it helps to imagine that you are releasing anxiety with each exhalation and welcoming peace with each inhalation. Once you feel a sense of calm or stillness, take a few moments to think of somewhere that represents a beautiful, peaceful, safe place to you. It may be somewhere you already know and love, or you may want to create an imaginary safe place. In whatever form it takes, this is an internal safe place for *you*. No one can enter unless you invite them. This includes your vicious inner voice or any thoughts that don't serve and support you.

Now see this safe place clearly in your mind's eye. Look around you. Notice what the sky looks like, what you can hear going on around you, and what you can smell. Bend down and touch the earth. Take up a handful of soil (or whatever it is for you) and feel it trickle through your fingers. What colour is the soil? What texture is it? Breathe in feelings of safety and support. Invite these feelings to come alive within you. Stay with it as these feelings of safety and support grow. Notice if things are changing as you strengthen your connection with your safe place.

Visit your safe place regularly. Each time notice how things have may have evolved. For instance, a stream may have appeared, or clouds in the sky may have cleared, or more birds and animals have arrived.

Using visualisation like this is a bit like going to the gym. We need to go regularly to build up muscle tone. Apply the same technique to your safe place. If you continue to find it difficult to visualise your safe place, draw a picture of it or write about it and pin it up where you can always see it.

How to use your safe place

Visit your safe place any time you need to draw on inner strength, courage, and resilience. Or you can just hang out in your safe place when you want to escape the rigour of life, or when you want a few minutes to relax during a hectic day. You can also ask your safe place for clarity over an issue that is bothering you, or what a difficult situation may be teaching you.

My own safe place is a beautiful ancient woodland clearing with the sound of a crystal-clear stream tumbling over stones nearby. I have a large canvas hammock strung between gnarled trunks of two magnificent oak trees in full summer leaf, in which Dooey (my beloved black fur-ball of a cat, who was killed by a car four years ago) waits for me, luxuriously stretched out in dappled sunlight. I intend to be in my safe place as I enter my dying process. I can't think of anywhere I would rather be.

Defusing negative feelings (I use this method frequently)

When you are struggling with low self-worth, anxiety or any negative core belief and want to step away from what it's doing to you, light a candle and sit in a chair or lie down somewhere comfortable.

Focus on slowing down your breath as you allow these negative or painful feelings to surface. I usually say something like, "Come on then, come and get me!' This may sound alarming but negative beliefs or feelings won't kill you. They just stop you from enjoying life and being at peace with who you are.

So be brave. Allow the feelings to intensify. Keep focusing on your breath and reminding yourself that you are doing this for yourself, and for everyone you know and love. As the feelings continue to intensify, you may find yourself automatically releasing negativity through your outbreath, and you may feel an urge to cry or to sob.

Crying and sobbing is a healthy release of the distress that you are carrying in your body. Sobbing won't kill you either. It may feel as if you are out of control, but the body has a miraculous way of keeping you safe. Your sobbing will start to lessen as you release your pain, and then a sense of peace and relief becomes present.

You may also release memories that you have buried deep in your subconscious. What surfaces may be uncomfortable, but, again, they won't kill you. They hold the secret for what prevents you from dying consciously.

Mindfully relax into whatever is happening for you and just keep breathing until these thoughts and feelings peak. Then enjoy the relief that follows. Name this new sensation as a positive core belief. For example, 'I am healing.' 'I am open to healing.' 'I am finding new ways to live more fully.' 'Right now, I feel peaceful.'

I always make sure that I take care of myself after I have done this kind of inner work. I will either take a bath with lots of lovely aromas, or book a massage, or go for a walk, or dance my socks off. I also write what I have experienced in my diary. This reminds me of my progress as I continue along my path to spiritual wellbeing. As I have said already, you may need to repeat this exercise a lot. But that's okay. Every time you release even the smallest amount of negativity you are building up resilience.

The cosmic shower

As with the method above, allow the negative core beliefs and feelings to emerge and intensify. Take several long, slow breaths and imagine you are standing under a powerful shower and feel these negative thoughts being washed away. See all that blackness disappearing down the plug hole. Experience how clean and fresh you feel as you step out of the shower. Don't feel despondent if the negative feelings rush back in. Just step back under the shower again until you feel that something has shifted.

The screen method (particularly helpful for intrusive shame attacks)

Imagine you are holding the remote control for a huge television screen in front of you. Project what you are feeling onto the screen. Hold the image for a moment then consciously press the off button. If the image reappears, press the off button again. If you are unable to turn the screen off, push a button that changes the channel or whatever else your imagination tells you do.

Turning feelings into an image

This is a simple NLP (Neurolinguistic Programming) technique that I use frequently. Allow your negative feeling or belief to build in strength, then turn it into a shape, texture and colour. It may help to draw or write down what you are experiencing. Create the clearest image possible in front of you. Then command it to move away from you. Imagine the image decreasing in size as it moves further away, then see it 'slide' through the wall or window and disappear.

If it refuses to move away, you can change what you are seeing into an animal, bird, fish or insect and give it a name. It could turn into a terrified caged bird cringing in a corner, or a stampeding bull raging with frustration, or a foundering fish, or a struggling butterfly pupa. Talk to it. Ask it what it wants from you. Work out a way to calm it. Your inner 'Me' will help you.

Once you've got the hang of this, you can defuse negative thoughts and feelings anywhere, anytime. I've done it while standing in a supermarket queue, walking along the street, having dinner with friends, taking care of my grandchildren, and sitting on my own. The important thing is not to give up. Keep practising and you will be surprised at how simple it is to help yourself.

Knowing your truth

One of the most valuable ways of knowing your truth is to listen to the synergy or discord between what you are saying out loud and what you are feeling in your heart. If the words coming out of your mouth are aligned with what you are feeling in your heart, then you know this is your truth. However, if your mouth is saying 'Yes' and your heart is saying 'No' (or your mouth is saying 'No' and your heart is saying 'Yes') then STOP! It's time to consider what's *really* right for you.

All too often we ignore this simple inner knowing and end up in a right old mess. Or maybe it simply isn't the right time to make a decision. Sometimes the stress of sitting with uncertainty can feel overwhelming. Just know that the right decision will appear at the right time, and always bear in mind that whatever decision you make will have consequences for what happens next. It's best not to rush into something until your mouth and heart come into alignment.

Saying sorry

We have all said or done things that we wish we hadn't. Remorse is a healthy emotion, which prompts us to take responsibility for the hurt we have caused. It comes from the Latin root *re* for again, and *mordere,* to bite. When we feel remorseful it means what we have done is biting back at us. It gnaws at us until we do something to put things right. However, we can't force someone to forgive us. Nor is it appropriate to continue to beat ourselves up about what's happened.

When we feel we want to reach out to say sorry, it's essential we are clear about taking responsibility for our part in what happened. This does not include making excuses for how we behaved or trying to change history: it's about speaking from the heart. Should the other person not respond, stay open to the possibility that they may want to at some point in the future.

Saying sorry can be done by letter, email, through social media, through an intermediary or by a miraculous coincidental meeting. This happened to me several years ago when I was mooching around a town centre that I had never visited before. I wandered into a shop and, straight in front of me in the aisle, was someone with whom I had fallen out in the past. We looked at each other warily. Then we smiled at each other and, rather than walk away, we spent a little while catching up on our lives. I felt freed up when we parted company. It suggested to me that the Universe is always looking for ways to create harmony in our lives.

If you both agree to meet to find a resolution, be mindful of what may happen and keep yourself safe. For example, you may end up hearing some pretty harsh truths about yourself. Therefore, it may be better to have an impartial third-party present to witness your meeting and to protect either of you from causing further upset.

Saying sorry can be really hard because we have to swallow our pride and admit we were wrong, but it reminds us that we are human and fallible and that we have a lot to learn as we pass through our earthly existence.

If the other person (or you find yourself doing this) persists in blaming or judging or becomes abusive or refuses to take responsibility for their part in what happened, find a way to extricate yourself. Sometimes a relationship or friendship has reached an impasse. It's then down to whether you decide there's anything left to salvage, or you walk away.

Forgiving is not forgetting

To fully accept our mortality, we have to learn about forgiveness – not just to forgive those who have hurt us, but also to forgive ourselves.

The Forgiveness Project[29] is, for me, one of the most inspiring concepts I have encountered. Founded in 2004 by journalist Marina Cantacuzino, it provides a chance for people to overcome unresolved grievances so they can move on from harm or trauma and, in doing so, build a climate of tolerance, resilience, hope and empathy.

The project shows us all how forgiveness teaches us humility and compassion. However, during my long journey through life to find out who I am, I have struggled with some expectations of forgiveness. I have read many articles and books that say forgiveness should be unconditional, and, if we can't look the person in the eye and reach that depth of forgiveness, we continue to cause ourselves harm.

In my experience, forgiveness can consist of many complex levels. For example, when I thought I had finally let go of difficult feelings about a person, I was confronted by another layer of painful thoughts and feelings, which surfaced several years later, triggered by what a mutual friend told me. So, for me, the forgiveness process continued, and, to some extent, still continues. I find it comforting to know that other people also consider forgiveness an ongoing process.

Stephanie is in her late forties. She has two children and works in the healing arts. This is how she described the on-going journey of forgiveness with her mother:

> During a therapy session I found myself regressing to around the age of four. I was standing at the bottom of the stairs staring up at my parents who were having a ferocious argument at the top of the stairs. I remember pleading with them, 'Please stop. If you love me, you wouldn't be shouting at each other.' They took no notice of me, so I was left feeling terrified, unheard and unseen. My father eventually left us, and, even though he had mental health issues, I blamed my mother. I had to find a way to forgive her for that. But then she told me that when she had been pregnant with me, she had drunk a bottle of gin and thrown herself down the stairs. I found that incredibly hard to forgive. I try my best with her, but our relationship has always been difficult. I am very grateful that I have done this amount of work on myself so that

we can continue to have a relationship, and I
can continue to find forgiveness.

Some of us have been subjected to such cruel and
appalling behaviour that it is impossible to 'just
forgive'. This is why I am particularly drawn to the
teachings of Jack Kornfield, Buddhist teacher and
author of *The Path with Heart*, who writes about
forgiveness as an expression of compassion and
easing of the heart. He says that forgiveness is not
about justifying or condoning harmful actions and
nor do we need to seek out those who have caused
us harm. He suggests it's okay if we choose never
to see the person again. The most important thing
is to find a way to ease our heart so we don't shut
the person out of our heart. He states, 'We have all
been harmed, just as we have all, at times, harmed
ourselves and others.'

I felt liberated when I read this because it gives
me permission to step away from the expectation of
having to sit across the table eyeball to eyeball with
a person who has triggered immense hurt and pain
in me. Rather, I can work on my forgiveness as a
heart opening practice for the person, myself and
the entire human condition. I find this very healing.

A Forgiveness Exercise

Here is a forgiveness exercise (adapted from other
forgiveness exercises), which I use in my workshops:

Choose one person or situation at a time. You can also choose yourself as part of your own self-forgiveness process.

1st step: ask yourself if you are ready to make the choice to forgive this person (or yourself). If not, ask yourself whether you are able to see a time in the future when you might be willing to make this choice.

2nd step: be aware that the act of forgiveness is not an event. It is a process, sometimes life long.

3rd step: be aware of what stops you from entering into the process of forgiveness with this person, situation, or yourself. It may be due to fear of letting go. Resentment may have become part of your personality, your reason for living, your need to get even. Or, be aware that acts such as extreme bullying, cruelty, abuse, rape, and torture are beyond your present ability to forgive. Sometimes we need to seek specialist help to start the forgiveness process.

4th step: be brave enough to recognise whether your forgiveness is a magnanimous gesture which makes you feel superior rather than one that genuinely comes from the heart. I have heard a number of people say that they have forgiven someone, but there's something about their tone of voice or the language they use that doesn't sound genuine.

Good listening skills

Throughout this book I have been talking about the importance of listening. This is another key to developing spiritual wellbeing.

The skills of good listening are about creating a safe, open and receptive space for another person to explore what they want to say without fear of being interrupted, fixed, judged, or the listener switching the attention back to themselves. Rather, we make gentle eye contact with them and become present as a benevolent witness for the person to work out what is going on for them. This means putting aside our own issues and agendas and giving our full attention. Often, we need to do little more than nod in affirmation as the person begins to have insights, which help them to see the truth for what it is, or a solution suddenly pops into their head.

How often have you experienced such unconditional listening skills? My guess is not very often, if ever.

Good listening is a gift of kindness and compassion. And I am continually surprised by the response from workshop participants after they have completed a good listening exercise. One participant, with tears in her eyes, said she had never been listened to like this before. Another said, 'I didn't realise what listening was. I thought it was talking to each other. But, I now realise, most people talk *at* each other.'

One participant in her mid-sixties had a profound emotional reaction following an exercise for deep inner listening. This simply involved placing her hand on her heart, focusing on her breath and listening to how her body responded. She said she had never done anything like this before. 'I had no idea that I could 'listen' to myself. It feels very weird but it's also very comforting. But I am so sad that it's taken me all these years to know it's possible.'

We know when we are in the presence of a poor listener. They either overwhelm us with a barrage of words, seldom drawing breath, or they regale us with their endless dramas and stories, or they talk over us, or constantly turn the conversation back to themselves, or they start glancing at their phone or fiddling with their watch when we start to talk, or they preach at us, know better than us, lecture us, try to fix us, make a joke out of what we are saying, or start to yawn.

Poor listening by others makes us feel invisible, unworthy of having our own experiences, and very resentful. And, when we fail to listen to ourselves, this is what we create as our inner life. If you want an example of poor listening, tune into Prime Minister's question time. It's shameful.

Good listening guidelines

There are some simple guidelines to good listening which can be life changing. Sometimes it's a good idea to set a space of time (for example, ten minutes) for one person to speak without being interrupted, followed by a short break. Then it's the turn of the other person to speak uninterrupted.

- Be respectful – allow the person to express their own views. It doesn't matter if you disagree. It's just a differing viewpoint, which isn't going to kill you!
- Be honest – own your personal experience. Speak from your heart. Use language such as 'I felt this when such and such happened.' Stay away from accusatory language such as, 'You did this, or you said that.'
- Be receptive – engage body language which shows that you are listening. Make eye contact whenever possible. Listen to their tone of voice. Beware of changes to their skin and facial colour and their willingness to engage with you.
- Be intuitive – are they saying what they really mean? Is their body language or facial expression saying something different from their words?
- *Be present* – it's very easy for your attention to become hijacked by thoughts or fears about the person. Or your mind drifts to a list of tasks that has to be completed. On the other hand, an unbidden memory may suddenly pop into your head, taking away your focus. Or what the person is talking about triggers an unresolved issue for you or you find you are relating strongly with what they are saying. Consciously take a breath to bring yourself present again.

- Be aware of your feelings – you may be feeling embarrassed by intimacy or afraid that the other person may cry; or you feel the need to fill any silences. Breathe slowly to calm yourself.
- Be open – you may find out things about each other that you never knew before. This knowledge can bring you closer.
- Be grounded – feel your feet firmly on the floor. This position will help you to be present and accepting of how things are unfolding.
- Finally, allow the silences to do their work. It's often the time when people have profound insights.

Creating synergy

All this work we do on ourselves creates synergy. As I wrote about in my introduction, I have been particularly inspired by the teachings of Elisabeth Kubler-Ross, which uses the four quadrants model to explain how synergy or integration brings spiritual wellbeing and wholeness into our lives.

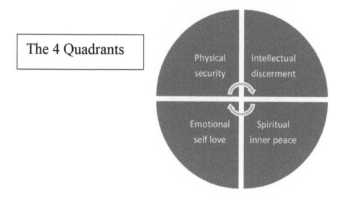

The 4 Quadrants

Physical
security

Intellectual
discerment

Emotional
self love

Spiritual
inner peace

Physical quadrant

Our body provides our emotional, intellectual and spiritual quadrants with a physical home as we pass through this life. It enables us to experience our five senses and to interrelate with the physical world. Its purpose is to provide us with physical growth, health and security – we need our body to survive. When we are disconnected from our body, we develop many fears, particularly around physical harm. When we feel comfortable in our body, we develop inner security.

Emotional quadrant

Neuroscience now suggests that our emotional quadrant is influenced from inception. Emotions and feelings allow us to form healthy relationships.

In order to thrive, we need to feel that we belong, we love, and we are loved. Emotional immaturity creates feelings of panic, fear and stress. A healthy emotional quadrant promotes self-love and self-respect.

Intellectual quadrant

The intellectual quadrant continues to develop until we are around 25 years old. It gives us the ability to think and reason in order to survive. We all have an innate need to know – to make sense of things so our life has meaning. Intellectual immaturity or distortion makes us feel stupid, dumb, mad and inadequate. A healthy intellectual quadrant gives us good judgement, discernment, and the desire to learn more.

Spiritual quadrant

Our spirituality is said to develop around adolescence (although I believe that younger generations are demonstrating spiritual awareness at an earlier age these days). Its function is to connect us with our intuition and the 'Me' who we really are. It also enables us to reflect on the deeper questions of life and to the sense that we are part of something greater than just ourselves. Spiritual numbness or denial can lead to confusion, a lack of fulfilment, disconnection and emptiness. Spiritual maturity generates acceptance, inner peace and wellbeing.

If we can't live, how can we die?

Most of us, I imagine, will connect with the physical, emotional and intellectual sides of who we are. But some of us may not identify with a spiritual (or transpersonal) quadrant. I certainly had no idea that I had a spiritual quadrant until I began my healing journey.

Elisabeth Kubler-Ross's teachings taught me how essential it is to develop a mature spiritual quadrant in order to deal with our fear of dying. Our spiritual quadrant, she explains, enables us to take care of unfinished business, which keeps us from accepting our mortality. 'If we can't live, how can we die? If we can't die, how can we live?'

I believe spiritual maturity requires faith in unknown mystery. The word faith brings up strong reactions in many people who have been scarred by religious dogma or abused by those in religious authority. However, for me, the word faith is about a belief in the mystery and myth of being connected to something far greater. Mark Hederman, a Benedictine monk from Glenstal Abbey in Ireland, speaks in his book, *Living the Mystery,* about the way that mythic intelligence is an essential part of human understanding. He quotes theologian David Tacey, saying that no amount of modernisation can get rid of the language of myth. It is how the psyche speaks.

Yet, as Mark Hedeman points out, our conditioning 'has made us enemies of the spirit.' This, he says, drastically affects our relationship with any sense of life after death and, sadly, this is where many of us find ourselves.

I find it sad, too. I would argue that without faith we have no ritual. Without ritual we cease to experience the sacredness of life. Without the sacredness of life, fear of the unknown – especially death – becomes the filter for how we experience life.

I feel this is the right note on which to bring this chapter to a close. As I have said throughout this section, if you are struggling with life or you are terrified of death, do seek help and support from someone you feel comfortable with, or join a group, workshop or organisation that you trust. I believe we are constantly being called to engage with our spiritual wellbeing so we can accept our mortality. When we open up to this, we are often mysteriously and miraculously led to those who can hold a space for us to confront our fear of death.

I interviewed Paul Wilson, who is strategic lead for prevention, mental health and wellbeing (adult community health services for people in Bristol, North Somerset and South Gloucestershire), about the importance for all us to develop self-care so we can support ourselves and each other through difficult times.

Speaking as a Welshman, Paul is very proud of the lead that Wales has taken in recognising the importance of wellbeing as a measure of national success. In 2015, the Welsh Assembly passed the Wellbeing of Future Generations Act. The Act contains seven wellbeing goals to make Wales a more equal, healthier, resilient and globally responsible country. New Zealand's government has recently enacted similar legislation and produced a 'wellbeing budget', focusing not only upon GDP (gross domestic product) but also upon GWB – general wellbeing.

If I am asked what causes mental health problems – a subject about which it is unwise to generalise – I usually feel safe enough in saying, 'The bad things that happen to people and the good things that don't.' That response recognises both the impact of trauma upon our lives and the equally debilitating effect of unmet human needs. It is the latter that I tend to focus upon in my work, by promoting the importance of wellbeing.

Human beings – despite their undoubted individuality – share certain universal needs. If these needs are not met, there will be adverse psychological and emotional reactions. As these reactions become more severe we call them mental health problems. Governments have a responsibility to meet these needs, but so do we, as individuals. Wellbeing offers us a way – indeed several ways. By embracing them we can improve the quality of our lives and reduce demand upon health services. At a personal level, wellbeing is empowering. It offers us proven ways of meeting important human needs – e.g. by being connected to others, staying active, taking notice of what is going on around us, continuing to learn and giving to others. These are not state services, it is important to note, but daily practices that are free to all citizens at all times. And they are relevant from our first breath to our last. By adopting them we leave a legacy of love and care – for ourselves and also for others. Indeed, it is by caring for others that we can become motivated to take better care of ourselves – even in very serious situations.

I remember a young woman who reduced her intake of food down to twice a week. You know what's going to happen when someone does something so extreme to themselves. But she was introduced to the concept of wellbeing and she began to start eating more frequently so that she would have the energy to help others to learn about wellbeing and practise it, too. Wellbeing gave profound meaning and purpose to her life. It turned her pain into her best qualification to help others. The appreciation she received from others increased her self-worth. And because she cared more about herself, she took better care of herself. A new and stronger person was born.

By practicing wellbeing and engaging in pro-social acts we also amass and share true wealth; a currency of incalculable value ... love. By adding to the common store of this most exalted emotion – to the commonwealth, as it was once known – we Each create a lasting legacy. So when death comes to find us, we will always be ready to embrace her and account for ourselves, because we know our time on earth has been well spent.

I know that my name will not enter the history books. I will never be rich. Nor will I be famous. I do not care about such things. I consider them false measures of success. Instead, I tell my family and friends how much I love them every day. More importantly I show them. I try to demonstrate love and respect for strangers, too; and for the creatures that are unfortunate enough to share this planet with us; and for the planet itself – our beautiful, long-suffering mother. That will be my legacy. It is enough.

As Paul says, practising wellbeing empowers us with choice and helps us to walk our path of truth. Once we connect to who we are, we start to go beyond our mundane, everyday existence and make room inside ourselves to open up to the transpersonal.

This is what we are going to explore in the next part of the book.

SECTION 3:

THE TRANSPERSONAL

CHAPTER 9

WE ARE MUCH MORE THAN WE THINK WE ARE

~

Even as a child I felt there was far more to me than just a body and a rather out of control mind. I also knew instinctively that I was going to die one day. However, similar to many baby boomers, I was brought up in a family and educated at a Church of England school where Christianity was obligatory, and spirituality was an anathema. Consequently, I went through my childhood rejecting a God who I couldn't relate to, and devoid of a spiritual inner life that could help me to understand who I was.

This had serious consequences on my ability to mature into a responsible adult or to form successful relationships. Fortunately, I eventually found a therapist whose kindness and compassion inspired me to train as a therapist as part of my spiritual journey (many counsellors and psychotherapists enter this field because of a need to heal their wounds and explore who they are).

During my training, I was introduced to Abraham Maslow's Transpersonal Psychology. Maslow is best known for his 'Hierarchy of Needs' pyramid symbol, which illustrates that once we have our basic physical needs met for us – to feel safe and secure (shelter, food and clothing) – we can draw on our evolving potential to develop a sense of love, belonging, intimacy, acceptance and trust. This, in turn, generates self-esteem and infuses respect in others and for others. Maslow recognised that it is only when we have established these external and inner resources that we can eventually self-actualise.

Maslow describes self-actualisation as an inherent desire 'to become everything one is capable of becoming.' Yet, he also recognised that human nature likes to be comfortable. However difficult or stressful their life may be, many people, either consciously or unconsciously, choose to remain in a comfort zone that meets their immediate needs (e.g a relationship/family/job/status) rather than continue with the process of self-actualisation. I certainly know a number of people who choose to stay put rather than stir the self-actualisation pot. I empathise with them. It takes effort, dedication and often-painful inner work and sacrifice to realise our full potential.

Transcendence

Before his death in 1970, Maslow began to grasp that there was a higher state to self-actualisation, which he considered to be still ego-attached. He called this higher state 'self-transcendence' or 'high-plateau experience' – going beyond any sense of the individual self ('I'-personality) or ego.[30]

A high-plateau experience is to reach a state of being when our experiences of life are just what they are. There's no interpretation, no drama, no constructing stories, no indulgence, no attachment and no embellishments. Entering a high-plateau experience also takes us beyond our history, environment, upbringing, and political and societal expectations. Again, this is not about demolishing our ego. Rather, we are no longer unconsciously controlled by it.

Reaching a high-plateau experience seems to be an incredibly tall order, but, as Dr Jeffery Martin reports in his fascinating book *The Finders,* his fourteen-year research study, into what makes people content, illustrates how thousands across the world have somehow put a stop to the endless negative chatter in their heads, and shifted from soul searching and goal setting into this high plateau experience. Jeffry Martin calls it Fundamental Wellbeing: realising peace of mind.

Transpersonal Therapy

Maslow recognised that people in distress require a holistic approach to healing, which acknowledges and addresses the spiritual or intangible aspects of who we are. Therefore, his transpersonal therapeutic model draws on profound transcendent philosophies, religious teachings and spiritual practices while, at the same time, remaining open to new consciousness expanding perceptions to help people to find their true place in the world and to see the bigger picture.

For Maslow, the bigger picture puts mortality at the centre of human spirituality and views death as an important transition. He reasoned that the fragility of life teaches us profound gratefulness, acceptance, assuredness, love, compassion, and a deep sense of faith and connection to something greater. Its appeal inspired me to find a transpersonal therapist when I began to question deeply who I was.

The transpersonal model

This particular interpretation of the transpersonal model was explained to me by the wonderful transpersonal therapist who supported me. It outlines how we come into this life carrying three essential elements:

- The DNA of our parents and ancestors, which affects what we look like, how we develop in life and influences what may happen to us through certain ancestral predispositions.
- Our entire human evolutionary story, which is carried in our cellular structure, dating back tens of thousands of years. Therefore, each one of us carries the entire narrative of human life on Earth within us.
- And something completely unique, which shapes our personal life experiences.

From this model I understand that there are certain things which we can't change. For example, I can't change the fact that I am a white female, born into a middle-class Western culture during the mid-twentieth century, influenced by the genetic imprint of my ancestors. The development of DNA technology

177

is now showing us why we may exhibit particular talents, habits and gifts as well as certain character traits – both positive and negative – which have been passed on to us genetically.

Also, I understand that we are part of a much richer picture, which connects us to the entire evolution of the human condition. Therefore, I consider that we are all fundamentally connected through our cellular structure to the natural world, which continues to sustain our evolving human story as it has done for millennia. We are part of nature, and nature is part of us. I am deeply moved by the way Brian Cox describes, in his BBC series *Wonders of the Universe,* how each one of us is destined to return to the same stardust that made us in the first place.

At the same time, we carry a completely unique energetic 'programming', which means that no other human being will *ever* experience life in exactly the same way as we do.

I consider this uniqueness to be created through the relationship between our biological DNA blueprint and what I term as our transpersonal blueprint. I believe our transpersonal blueprint takes us beyond biology by energetically drawing to us all of the experiences that we need to progress spiritually during our lifetime so we can heal the wounds of our ancestors which have been passed onto us. I regard this to be a fundamental task for every one of us. Chilean author Isabel Allende writes:

We don't know what we carry on the inside.
We don't only carry genes: there are spiritual
genes as well. Many people believe that we
carry our ancestors' vices and their virtues.
I believe that we carry their spiritual legacy
as well.'

Our biological blueprint

The biology of our DNA unquestionably plays
an important role in shaping us into who we are,
and it's incredibly exciting to learn that biological
science is now discovering how our DNA creates
the blueprint of who we are. So, it's timely to pay
homage to James Watson and Francis Crick who
discovered Deoxyribonucleic acid (DNA), in 1953,
as a molecule consisting of two chains that twist
round themselves to form a beautiful double helix.

Basically, our DNA (which is carried in all
organisms and many viruses) is programmed with
genetic instructions for how we develop, function,
grow and reproduce. It does not construct our
bones or make us run and jump or scream and
yell. But it does contain all the information or
coding, which our body requires for building
essential proteins that make this happen, and
for each cell's development, reproduction and
ultimate death.[31]

This is why DNA is called the blueprint of
life. I suppose you could describe it as our own

personal computer software. Dr David Goodsell, associate professor of the Scripps Research Institute in California, produces extraordinary graphics[32] of how our DNA holds around 25,000 genes that make up our individual genetic code, and how DNA can miraculously heal itself.

Apparently, it's difficult to estimate how many cells we have in our body because cells come in different sizes and grow in different densities. But it is possible that we may have over seven trillion. Each one of these cells normally contains 23 pairs of chromosomes (totalling 46), which store our genetic information and are made from DNA.

Interacting through our DNA

Our *entire* cellular structure carries our personal DNA blueprint of life. In his book *The Divine Matrix*, Gregg Braden explains how we interact with our environment *through* our DNA, which, he says, is vibrating with a frequency that communicates with what some quantum physicists refer to as the Quantum Field.[33]

Quantum physicists theorise that a pure state of nothing does not and cannot exist. We are surround by an invisible quantum field or force field that contains no physical particles and registers at a temperature of zero, but subatomic particles (minute portions of matter which cannot be seen by the naked eye) still emanate some kind of wave-like vibrations or energy.

Therefore, in the terms of quantum physics, nothing can't exist.[34]

This quantum theory has laid the scientific groundwork for attempting to explain how our thoughts are waves of energy, which interact with the Quantum Field and cause physical things to manifest in our lives. Quantum physics is an incredibly complicated, brain-aching area of research, which requires mega grey matter to go any further. My grey matter has wisely decided to leave it here for now.

Epigenetics

I am also fascinated in how ground-breaking research into epigenetics (the study of our biological mechanisms that switch genes on and off) is now suggesting that we are not victims to our genetic make-up. We can actually change our DNA by changing our thoughts.[35] Studies by the Centre for Addiction and Mental Health in Toronto, on patients with schizophrenia and bipolar disorder, indicate that mental illness is not hereditary. Rather, it is co-created with the environment surrounding the patient. For example, a negative environment co-creates negative thoughts. A positive environment co-creates positive thought. To me this sounds obvious, but it's good that science is giving it backbone.

A team of epigenetic scientists, working with the Heartmath Institute, has also published findings on the way that what we think and feel influences our genetic blueprint. In one experiment, selected participants were able to change their DNA with positive mental states.[36] I find this research to be incredibly empowering. It means that every one of us has the ability to change what isn't working for us. We just need to learn to apply ourselves.

Our transpersonal blueprint

I believe that our biological blueprint is energetically interwoven with what I have described as our transpersonal blueprint. I need to say that the following description of this transpersonal blueprint is formed by my own perceptions after years of reflecting on what makes each one of us such unique individuals. I realise this may be a stretch for some readers but keeping an open mind maintains the possibility of considering something new and different.

In spiritual or religious terms, transpersonal energies can be referred to as the spirit or soul. Eastern practices and many indigenous traditions also believe we are greatly influenced by fate, destiny and karma. Many people dismiss fate, destiny and karma as New Age concepts. All I know is that life relentlessly challenges us to find out who we really are. So, personally, I accept that something multidimensional is going on inside me that shapes my life and calls me to become, in the words of Abraham Maslow, 'everything I am capable of becoming'. This is not a biological calling. This comes from a far deeper transpersonal place.

For the sake of clarity, I present each transpersonal energy individually. However, when I visualise transpersonal energies, I see ribbons of colour, like a translucent rainbow, dancing through our biological blueprint. One blueprint cannot be separate from the other or, indeed, from any other system within our cellular makeup.

We'll start with spirit and soul, principally because most people are aware of both concepts. Spirit and soul are often referred to as the same thing, but many religions view them differently. Some traditions, such as Buddhism, do not believe in the existence of 'soul;' (for Buddhists there is no permanent self or soul) although along with most religions, it recognises the transcendent nature of spirit.

The Spirit: Transcending

Spirit comes from Latin *spiritus*, meaning 'breath' [of life]. The New Testament explains the spirit as that which gives life to a body, and, without spirit, the body is dead (James 2:26). In Hindu sacred texts, the Suetasuatara Upanishad Part 3 calls the spirit Atman: 'Concealed in the heart of all beings lies the Atman, the Spirit, the Self; smaller than the smallest atom, greater than the greatest space.'

Some people refer to the spirit as our internal flame, our higher being, The God Within, our True Self. Others describe it as our guiding light, our source of Love and joy, our divine goodness, our

Divinity. Thomas Moore, author of *Dark Nights of the Soul*, describes the spirit as the part of us that wants to transcend.

I know the feeling of wanting to transcend. It's as if something is constantly pressing me to go beyond the dramas of life so I create room inside myself for the Love of the Universe to come into physical form. This Love is what the third century Persian poet Rumi describes as the call of the Beloved. When I connect with this call of the Beloved, the banality of life fades away and a much stronger sense of who I am steps forward. Whatever our spirit is, I see it as the part of us that can never be destroyed, coerced or corrupted. It is the pure part of who we are. For me, it's my God within.

The Soul: Attaching

'Soul' comes from Old English *sáwol,* originally meaning 'coming from or belonging to the sea or lake' (perhaps symbolic of our psyche or unconscious). The Bible explains the soul as the life, which a person or an animal has (1 Peter 3:20). Hindu scripture refers to the soul as 'Jivatman': 'In this vast wheel of creation wherein all things live and die, wanders round the human soul like a swan in restless flying, and thinks that God is afar' (Suetasuartara Upanishad: part 1).

Our soul, says Thomas Moore, needs a sense of home, and loves to attach to life. Jacob Nordby, author of *The Divine Arsonist – A Tale of Awakening,* considers that every one of our desires in an expression of our soul's longing to experience human life.

I take this to mean that our soul is driven to experience life in any way it can, even if this means living under extreme duress or suffering the worst that humanity can imagine. Certainly, our compulsion to be alive and stay alive is formidable. Perhaps it is the creative tension between the desire of our spirit to experience transcendence in physical form and our soul's overwhelming desire to attach to life that sparks our life force. It puts me in mind of Freud's concept that human beings possess an unconscious desire to die but our survival instincts largely alleviate this wish. To me, this tension often feels like walking a tight rope in strong winds, strung between two high-rise buildings.

Our soul's desire for physical attachment also prompts me to wonder if this is what makes the dying process so protracted. It's as if our soul resists leaving the body until the final moment so it can absorb every last drop of human experience possible. It's astonishing to witness how the body, at the moment of death, suddenly turns from containing some form of life force into an empty envelope. *Something* has departed. Some people argue that the spirit has left; for others, it's the soul. Perhaps the two are intrinsically interlinked and both depart together, arm in arm, like old comrades. It's something that I continue to contemplate, along with the possibility that our soul is 'programmed' to carry the transpersonal energies of our fate, destiny and karma, which shapes our personal life journey.

Fate: Accepting

Many people regard fate and destiny as interchangeable, but they appear not to be. Fate comes from Latin *fatum,* 'that which has been spoken'. There's a sense of the inevitable: something that can't be changed. In Greek mythology, three old women or the three fates sit together creating the destinies of all living beings. Clotho spins the thread of destiny, Lachesis doles it out, and Atropos severs the thread when the moment of death approaches. I find that quite a disturbing image.

Another way of looking at fate is to imagine we are all born with a metaphorical set of cards in our hand. We can't throw our hand in or exchange our cards, so we are stuck with this set of cards throughout our lifetime.

Influenced by the ancestral spiritual legacy that we carry, I believe that our hand of fate is programmed with energetic life themes, which we draw to us along our journey. For example, some people's life themes are about stability and family. For others, they are about freedom or social justice. Some people's life themes are about healing and caring, or building a business, or attaining fame. Others carry life themes, which rub up against war, incarceration, poverty, deprivation or mental health issues. Whatever they may be, it seems as if the potency of these life themes come alive as we connect with them and find ways to turn them into something that works for us.

This is how Anne connected to one of her major life themes. Anne is in her late thirties and works as a physiotherapist.

I realised I was having an identity crisis. I was constantly finding myself as the number two or the support to people who took the lead, knowing I could do better. I always felt uncomfortable with this but didn't know why. During a therapy session I began to explore what my life themes could be. I had never heard of life themes before, so it intrigued me. It sparked off a series of memories of how, as a child, I always took the lead. I was also head of pony camp and head prefect at school. It was a complete light bulb moment. My major life theme, I realised, is leadership! But I had become so brow beaten by life that I had forgotten it. So, I am now literally taking the lead in my life and have signed up for a leadership programme so I can take my work with wellbeing into businesses and industry.

Les Brown is a black American who says that just because fate doesn't deal us with 'the right cards,' it doesn't mean we should give up. It means we have to learn to play the cards we get to their maximum potential. He should know. He was labelled as 'educable mentally retarded' by his elementary teachers. But Les drew on whatever talents he had and, coupled with sheer determination, persistence and self-belief, he went beyond cleaning loos to become one of America's most respected motivational speakers.[37] I find his story utterly inspiring. Yes, like many of us, I may be holding a difficult set of cards this lifetime, but it doesn't mean I am a victim to them. I can learn to accept and work with the cards I hold and find ways to transform them into their best possible potential.

Destiny: Choosing

Destiny comes from Latin *destinata* (fem) make firm, establish. We may not be able to change fate, but we can *choose* to play our cards differently as we go through life. Spiritual teacher and author Paulo Coelho beautifully sums up the difference between fate and destiny by explaining that we can control our destiny but not our fate. He says, 'I believe we all have the choice as to whether we fulfil our destiny, but our fate is sealed.'

As far as Paulo Coelho is concerned, our destiny is about learning to use free will to draw out the full potential of what lies within our hand of fate. Some of us seem to be born with clear destiny choices. Elton John, for example, knew he was going to be a pianist by the time he was four. Laurence Olivier fell in love with acting at school. Ken Dodd spoke about seeing a comedian when he was very young and instantly knew he wanted to make people laugh. Dame Kelly Holmes was inspired to become an Olympian while watching the Olympics as a youngster.

Some people are equally driven, from an early age, to become doctors, scientists, academics, teachers, environmentalists, charity workers or adventurers. It appears their fate and destiny are in perfect alignment and everything seems to conspire to make this happen. The rest of us – I include myself in this – have a more varied life. I have lost count of the number of jobs I have had. But, when I look back, I can see how each working experience (however dull) created another building block for me to do what I do now. I also see how fate and destiny have brought into my life all manner of people who have somehow helped me (although it may not have felt like that at the time) to grow stronger and more resilient by stretching my head, my heart and my soul. As JRR Tolkien says, 'Not all those who wander are lost.'

Free will

The concept of fate and destiny raises interesting questions about free choice. Personally, I think there are limitations to the 'you can do/get anything you want,' message that many New Age self-empowerment books promote. For instance, I can't choose to be a brain surgeon. I don't have the academic credentials or the will to become a brain surgeon. Nor am I here to become a pop star, an astronaut or a chimney sweep. In other words, it's not my fate or destiny. But I have learnt, over the years, that I have complete free will in how I accept who I am, how I react or respond to what's happening in my life, how I view life, and how I behave.

I imagine that the scope of free will, which is available to me, is rather like walking through a long, fairly narrow valley. Somehow, I know that my fate lies in my valley and, if I climb out of the valley, I will be lost. The sheer sides of the valley set the boundaries for my life experiences. As I walk along my valley, life experiences continually present themselves to me. I have the free will to engage with them, ignore them, or resist them. I also have free choice to learn from my experiences, and to return to my path when I realise that I have been side-tracked by a piece of fool's gold, which caught my eye.

In short, when I become aware of the power of free will, I become more sensitive to what I am here to learn and more attuned with the way in which cause and effect moulds my life. In Eastern traditions, cause and effect is defined as karma.

Karma: attracting

Karma comes from the Sanskrit *karman* meaning action or effect. Most of us in the West learn about karma mainly through Eastern practices and beliefs. But this can be a complicated concept to understand. So, I turned to Graham Lever, a Tibetan Buddhist who has been practicing Mahayana Buddhism since 1990. Graham runs local dharma groups and sees himself as a Buddhist student who shares knowledge. Mahayana means The Great Vehicle, which comes from the Indian, Tibetan and Chinese traditions.

The Dalai Lama is the leader of the Tibetan branch of Mahayana.

Buddhism believes that there is much more to us than just our physical body. We are energetic beings who carry a white Light inside, which connects us to everything both physical and non-physical. Therefore, there is no separation. We are all an eternal part of each other. Erwin Schrödinger famously said that 'the total number of minds in the Universe is one'. The Buddhist might add, 'and that is Buddha-nature'.

Many in the West don't fully understand what karma means. It's not a bundle of 'stuff' that is destined to happen. It is the result of cause and effect. We describe karma as energetic seeds that may have been planted lifetimes ago, waiting for the right conditions in which to ripen. The western mind tends to be very linear in its attempt to understand the transcendent. It likes to put things into separate compartments. But it isn't like that. Everything is simultaneously interacting with everything else. It's a cosmic flow of consciousness that is outside the restrictions of human knowledge and time doesn't exist anyway.

We believe we don't spring out of nowhere. We are unconsciously blown into the most suitable rebirth by karmic winds in the Alaya consciousness. It can be a difficult concept to take on board, but I look at the Alaya as infinite high consciousness, which is very subtle and vast like an ocean.

If we have trained and studied well in meditation and lucid dreaming during our previous lifetime, we may have more awareness to direct matters in the post-mortem state [between lives]. Only then. So, in this sense, there is no 'death' but a continuum of consciousness when we leave this life. Yes, our thoughts and emotions may cease to exist, but the Alaya, which is the storehouse of our habits and karmic imprints and of our ground awareness of 'sparkling energy', continues.

The ancestral lineage, status and culture that we are born into is where we can learn what is most required. If the conditions are right, our karmic seeds germinate and draw to us the lesson that we need to release the limitations of fear, ignorance and attachment. If the conditions are not right, our karmic seeds remain dormant until the next rebirth. But everything is about free choice. From the moment we develop awareness, we have the choice of how we respond to what's happening, and every action we take has an effect. We call it awareness in the moment. That's all enlightenment is. Once we become aware, we burn off our karma forever. This is the action of the true Buddha nature.

We believe it is essential to meditate on death. This keeps us focused on what's important in life and keeps us connected to our heart. In Buddhism, the heart is the mind, which goes beyond words and takes us beyond the ego. It also makes us mindful of our karmic obligations.

I think about death every day. Not in a morbid way. Rather, I'm curious and positive about it. I want to have plenty of notice so I can say my goodbyes, and I am happy to die wherever it's easiest for my family, even if this means in hospital. I love how the artist William Blake died singing hymns. That puts death into perspective for me, and I constantly remind myself of the millions of people younger than me who have already died. At the age of 71, I find it a miracle that I'm still here, so I don't want to waste a single moment of life.

I find what Graham says uplifting and inspiring. It teaches me the importance of taking responsibility for who I am and to be aware that every action I take creates an effect. I love the concept of burning off karma forever. I see this as an essential part of preparing to die consciously.

To conclude this chapter, I have constructed a table of how I see the higher, aligned aspects of our transpersonal energies working together and what happens when we are closed or non-aligned with them.

When we are aligned there is a sense of transcending from the mundane to build a healthily attachment to life. This means accepting who we are, consciously making right choices and embracing the knowing of what we are here to learn and to heal.

Non-alignment is when we close down to these transpersonal energies. This dims our spirit, builds resistance to what life has to offer, and makes us reject and ignore what life is showing us. Yet our karma is constantly attracting situations and people into our life to wake us up. Therefore, while we still have breath in our body, we can never escape from ourselves.

As I reflect on how these transpersonal energies play out, I get the feeling that we are neither in complete control of our lives nor are we chess pieces in a preordained game plan. I like that.

TRANSCENDENT ENERGY	ORIGINAL MEANING	ALIGNMENT	NON ALIGNMENT
SPIRIT Spark of God or universal consciousness within us	LATIN *SPIRITUS*: BREATH	TRANSCENDING	DIMMING
SOUL Carries the energetic lessons we need to learn	OLD ENGLISH *SAWOL*: 'OF THE SEA'	ATTACHING	RESISTING
FATE Our set of cards this lifetime	LATIN *FATUM*: THAT WHICH IS SPOKEN	ACCEPTING	REJECTING
DESTINY How we choose to play these cards	LATIN *DESTINATA* (FEM) TO MAKE FIRM	CHOOSING	IGNORING
KARMA Draws life experiences to teach us about the laws of cause and effect	SANSKIT *KARMAN* CAUSE/EFFECT	ATTRACTING	ATTRACTING

In the next chapter we're going to explore how scientific discoveries in quantum consciousness are beginning to challenge our entire understanding of what living fully and dying consciously really means.

CHAPTER 10

THE UNIVERSE IS IN US

Even before Max Planck won the 1918 Nobel Prize for Energy Quanta and Albert Einstein imagined what might happen if he raced alongside a light beam (what a wonderful vision for the law of relatively), quantum consciousness has been a hot area of research. I should add that quantum consciousness is referred to in many different ways across many different disciplines. For example, the scientific community may call it The Quantum Field, The Unified Field or The Zero Point Field.[38] Religions refer to it as God, Brahma and The Supreme. Esoteric teachings call it Universal Intelligence, Universal Life Energy, the Light, The Source and Ultimate Love. For now, we're going to stay with quantum consciousness.

The quantum leap

There seems to be a lot of talk about 'quantum consciousness' and making a 'quantum leap' in the area of personal development, so this is my understanding of what it means.

'Quantum' comes from the Latin meaning *amount*.[39] Physics defines quantum movement as the sudden or smallest (or discrete) energetic change (or leap) from one energy state to another within an atom, made up of invisible sub-particles called protons, neutrons and electrons. So, in scientific terms, a 'quantum leap' has a different meaning from the momentous or evolutionary leap that has infiltrated our everyday language. This can be traced back to an essay written in 1956 by H. L. Robert in which he discusses the 'quantum leap' or escalation of nuclear weapons that, at the time, described the perilous American-Soviet power balance.

Quantum consciousness (also referred to as the quantum mind) defines a group of scientific theories suggesting that the classical mechanics of physics cannot clarify what consciousness actually is.[40] In other words, it doesn't possess the capacity to physically measure it and, therefore, prove it exists. However, quantum physicists and neuroscientists are now studying the possibility that quantum processes (those invisible leaps) play a role in the way we assimilate knowledge and understanding through our thoughts, experiences and senses – in short, through consciousness itself. I love how astrophysicist Neil deGrasse Tyson, who received the Stephen Hawking Science Medal in 2017, says, 'We are part of this Universe; we are in this Universe; but, perhaps more important than both of those facts, is that the Universe is in us.'

Christof Koch, chief scientific officer at the Allen Institute for Brain Science in Seattle, measures consciousness through something called Integrated Information Theory (IIT).[41] Koch says that evidence from his IIT studies suggests that the entire cosmos is immersed in consciousness and infused with ability to sense and feel and, therefore, is alive. He describes it as the air we breathe, the soil we tread on, the bacteria which colonizes our intestines and the brain that enables us to think.

Lynne McTaggart, author of *The Field* and innovator of Power of 8 groups, believes that if we could understand quantum consciousness scientifically, we might be able to tap into it systematically. This, she says, would vastly improve every area of our lives and help us to make the final evolutionary step in understanding our full potential. I'm with Lynne on this one. If we really are highly conscious beings radiating with quantum consciousness (as, in their own way, ancient civilizations and indigenous cultures have always believed us to be) then this puts a very different slant on what mortality actually means. In fact, to my mind, it scientifically changes our entire perception of life and death.[42]

Awaking into quantum consciousness

So how do we awaken into quantum consciousness?

First, we have to become aware of what we are creating in our life. Are we still driven by fear, dread, shame or yearning? Or are we choosing spiritual wellbeing to guide our life? Second, we have to step up to the work it takes to discipline our mind and open our hearts to something well beyond our present understanding of what life is.

Metaphysicians and esoteric teachers have been talking about this for a long time. One of my favourites is Baron Eugene Fersen, a wonderfully eccentric Russian aristocrat who arrived in America in 1902 with his mother, the Grand Duchess of Russia. In his book *The Science of Being,* published in 1923, he identifies Universal Life Energy as a primal vibrating force that creates manifest reality. But first, he says, we have to train our mind to be still, through silence and relaxation, in order to actualise this consciousness. Although few have heard of him today, the baron was one of the most revered and respected esoteric teachers of his time.

Around the same time, Earnest Holmes (I like to imagine that he and the baron took tea together on many occasions) founded Religious Science in America, which became part of the greater New Thought movement. Holmes was also a prolific writer and teacher for the science of the mind. One of his statements of belief is: 'I believe that the Universal Spirit, which is God, operates through a Universal

Mind, which is the Law of God; and that I am surrounded by this Creative Mind which receives the direct impress of my thought and acts upon it.'

The holon effect

I liken what Earnest Holmes says to the analogy of the holon. Holon comes from the Greek, meaning something that is simultaneously a whole and a part. One can't exist without the other yet there's a sense of autonomy at the same time. A holon is perfectly represented by the shape of a wheel. Each spoke is an individual part that makes up the wheel, while the rim provides the structure and containment enabling each spoke to do what it needs to do.

43

If one spoke cracks, the wheel can't function properly or breaks altogether. As far as I can see, this is exactly what's happening to our world right now. Too many human spokes have broken down, destroying the holon of humanity. This disintegration of what holds us together collectively, and supports us as individuals, has thrown our entire understanding of life and death into chaos.

I suggest that our experience of death would be so different if we all grasped the fact that the human holon represents how we are profoundly connected to each other, held in place by the 'rim' of universal consciousness, which we come to Earth to express in physical form. It would allow us to shift away from our ego-driven nonsense to experience lives full of wonder and appreciation before returning to where we have come from. It would certainly release our fear of death and help us to understand that universal consciousness is organically attuned to our transpersonal blueprints.

Language of the Universe

In my experience, universal consciousness speaks to us through the language of messages, which arrive out of nowhere in our head or as a feeling in our body. This could be a sudden vision or a premonition that something is going to happen. Or we might find ourselves called to do something quite different from what we are presently engaged in or to change our life completely. We may experience prophetic dreams that either give us a glimpse of the future or warn us about an event that actually happens.[44] We have the choice to act on these messages or not. I see this communication as a continual cycle of energetic exchange:

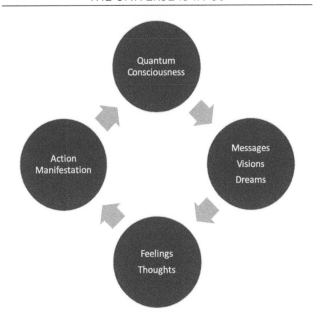

Our messages are channeled through our inspiration, instinct and intuition. People often classify these as the same thing, but I see each one as different.

Inspiration

Inspiration comes from the Latin *Inspirare,* literally meaning divine guidance. Jack Canfield, author of *Chicken Soup for the Soul,* describes inspiration as a satori – a sudden flash of insight, or sudden burst of creativity that can be life changing. It's the moment of revelation when the mind-fog clears and, suddenly, we see a situation or person for what they really are. Or it's the moment when the inventor receives the idea for a new product, or a writer suddenly gets the idea for their next novel; or the entrepreneur has a dream about a new business venture. But this flash of insight can be as slippery as an eel. Jack Canfield warns that if a new idea is not captured in 37 seconds it is likely never to be recalled again. And, in seven minutes it's gone forever. This is why I take a notebook and pen everywhere I go.

Instinct

Instinct comes from the Latin *instinctus,* meaning impulse. We are born with the instinct to survive. These are automatic or hard-wired reactions when we perceive danger and threat. Our instinct tells us to run away or warns us not to walk down a particular street; or we feel inexplicably uncomfortable around a particular person. Therefore, our instinct is not concerned with inspiring us or teaching us: it is concerned with our survival. 'When your own life is threatened,' writes Yann Martel, author of *The Life of Pi,* 'your sense of empathy is blunted by a terrible, selfish hunger to survive.'

Intuition

Intuition (in-tuition or inner teaching) comes from the Latin *intueri,* meaning to look inside or contemplate. Around 90% of the critical decisions that we make are based on intuition – a gift that we need to nurture and develop in order to make important decisions.[45] The simplest definition I have found is by Saraswami Ma, who writes in her book *I am I,* 'Intuition is knowing that you know, but not knowing *how* you know it.' I couldn't have put it better myself.

The Heartmath Institute, based in California, has been conducting extensive research into how intuition works, and suggests that intuition can be experienced in three ways:[46]

Implicit knowledge or learning

This refers to knowledge we have acquired in the past and may have forgotten. But our brain, in nanoseconds, has the ability to match the patterns of new issues we may be facing, with implicit memories of our past experiences, and come up with either a positive or negative emotional response that registers in our body. As such, our emotions and feelings are connected directly to our intuition.

Energetic sensitivity

Our nervous system is often affected by changes in geomagnetic activity. Therefore, energetic sensitivity refers to some people's ability to be able to forecast or have premonitions about changes in environmental signals such as electromagnetic fields. For example, sensing when an earthquake or a Tsunami is going to happen, or is about to happen.

Nonlocal intuition

This refers to the ability to sense or know about something that has not been experienced in the past and is not connected to environmental signals. The HeartMath Institute argues that we all have this ability because we are inherently interconnected with everything in the Universe. The examples they give are when a mother senses something is happening to their child even when the child lives on a different continent, or when people have a 'gut feeling' about making business decisions.

Blocked intuition

However, modern life is threatening our intuitive abilities. 'The intuitive mind is a sacred gift and the rational mind is a faithful servant. We have created a society that honours the servant and has forgotten the Gift,' said that wise genius Albert Einstein. This greatly concerns me. When we live in our head, we separate ourselves from the greater whole. We become over-dependent on technology, pack our minds with trivia, and believe that life out to get us.

But how can we believe we are separate beings when we experience those extraordinary coincidence and synchronicities, which often leave us open mouthed in amazement?

Coincidences

The definition of a coincidence is when two or more similar things happen at the same time, especially in a way that is unlikely and surprising. For instance, we've just been thinking about an old friend, and they appear as if by magic in the same railway carriage. Or we are on a beach in sunny Spain and glance up to see an old neighbour. Or we are thinking about a family member, the phone rings and we know it's them.

A coincidence happened to me not so long ago. I was browsing in a charity shop where I had lived fifteen years ago when a woman tapped me on the shoulder and said, 'Hello Sue.' In the next instance, another woman walked into the shop and stopped in surprise when she saw us both. All three of us had worked closely together for some years and left our place of work at similar times, but none of us had seen or been in touch with each other since. We retired to a teashop and had a wonderful catch up.

People often say that when coincidences happen you know you are on the right path. But the definition I like the most is by American author and playwright Laura Pederson, who says 'Coincidence is God's way of being anonymous.' When I experience these wonderful and miraculous coincidences, I often feel that 'God' is quietly laughing in delight.

Synchronicities

Synchronicities are different. Carl Jung, founder of analytical psychology who wrote extensively about the collective unconscious, was the first psychologist to consider that when events happen all over the world at the same time, they must be connected in some unknown way. This, he said, implies the presence of a deeper intelligence at work. For example, several unrelated scientists across the world may suddenly start to work on a similar scientific problem, which could benefit humankind. Or, all of a sudden, there's a pile of books being published on a particular self-development theme. Or several people simultaneously feel inspired to set up an Internet forum, which provides similar information, or start making a similar product. It's as if the Universe is downloading itself into anyone who will listen. It makes me wonder who really 'owns' an idea.

I am struck by the synchronistic political upheavals taking place across the globe at the present time. It feels as if these individual groups have connected on a much higher level to shake up worn out systems so a far more dynamic and integrated political world order can emerge. We don't know where all this upheaval is going at the moment, but I am expecting many more synchronistic uprisings to take place before we have clarity.

Head-heart-gut intelligence

The more we wake up to the mystery and magic of quantum consciousness, the more we instinctively become aligned with it. Research is now demonstrating how our entire body is programmed to do this through the intelligence of our head, heart and gut.

Dr Andrew Armour from Montreal University was the first scientist to introduce the term 'heart brain' in 1991. He identified that the heart's electromagnetic field is forty to sixty times stronger than the brain's electromagnetic field, and the heart sends more information to the brain than the brain sends to the heart. He also identified that when our mind and emotions are in alignment with our heart, there's is a flow of awareness, understanding, and intuition. As such, Armour defines the heart as our second brain, or 'little brain'.

The Heartmath Institute has been developing Armour's work and conducting extraordinary research into heart intelligence.[47] The Institute is aware of the immense changes that we are all facing globally and personally, and the urgency for us all to wake up and come into alignment with who we truly are through our heart intelligence.[48]

Gut intelligence

Justin Sonnenburg and Erica Sonnenburg's book *The Good Gut* explains how the primal connection between our brain, heart and gut provides us with gut feelings that help us to make instinctual choices which can actually save our lives, or to identify immediately with stressful situations (those sinking feelings) when we are confronted by something or someone we don't like, or a situation we don't want to experience. Therefore, our gut intelligence motives us into some kind of action. This emotive messaging between brain, heart and gut happens via the vagus nerve, the longest of our twelve cranial nerves, which is connected to all the organs and systems of our body[49].

There's a new movement called mBIT[50] (or mBraining) which teaches multiple brain integration techniques, developed by NLP trainers Grant Soosalu and Marvin Oka, authors of *Using Your Multiple Brains to do Cool Stuff*. The book is used as a guide to understand the scientific basis behind our gut intuition (courage), our heart-felt emotions (compassion), and our head-based creative powers (creativity). Well worth reading.

Katherine Brooke-MacKenzie is a colonic hydrotherapy practitioner who specialises in helping people to connect with their body intelligence. She came into this work following acupuncture treatment to give up smoking. It had such a profound effect on her mental and spiritual health that she studied it for three years. It laid a foundation in energy medicine that facilitated her to study colon hydrotherapy. Now, she says, she helps people to let go of – in her words – all the shit they are carrying so they can connect with themselves and to their life blueprint.

My work gives me the permission to explore the spiritual aspect of our gut. Inspiration arrives in our heart first. It then goes to the head so we can work out how to fulfil our ideas and desires. It goes back down to the heart and then to the gut where we draw on the courage and grounding to physically manifest things. We need our gut to do this. Otherwise there are plenty of good ideas out there but, unless we take them into our gut, they just stay as ideas. It's when the idea becomes a visceral experience that I know something is happening.

I also believe that we need to be persistent. If something doesn't work right away, we need to try again; and again, if necessary. It's about not giving up the goal, but listening to our head, heart and gut and being flexible along the way. I believe that a life well lived is paying attention to what's happening inside us as we go. Life and death are all about faith and trust.

I really resonate with the quote often attributed to Oscar Wilde that goes, 'Be yourself. Everyone else is taken.' I believe we are all born with our own blueprint. I see this as a straight line between heaven and earth, which passes through us. This blueprint is meant to carry us through our life. It sets out our path and draws to us all the learning we need to evolve as human beings.

But our blueprint gets bent out of shape by our parents' expectations, peer pressure and social pressures so we lose connection with the flow of who we are. This makes us fearful of change.

But I believe there's a matrix at work, which I call 'the soup of intelligence.' It's all there. It crosses over the world. There are lots of stories about people who can't do the crossword on Friday night. But when they wake up on Saturday morning they can. I love that.

I believe the essence of a person is to know what we are here for and that we are doing our bit to make things better. But I am also aware of another voice that says, 'Oh just get pissed instead.' So, for me, it's about honouring the fact that life can be an internal battleground and we need both the earthly and heavenly parts of us to come together and work together in healthy balance. To grow, we have to be prepared to take risks. That's part of our life experience. If we don't listen to our blueprint, we get ourselves into all sorts of trouble. That certainly happened to me. I completely threw myself away until I realised there was another way to life.

I want to die quietly. In fact, I have ordered my death! I see myself sitting on the side of my bed one day and I just step out of my body as if I am stepping out of my clothes. I don't want to have regrets when I die. And, I don't want to take any 'shoulds' and 'oughts' to my death either. We need to face this right now so when we reach our end, we're not thinking I wish I had done life differently.

This may sound a bit weird, but I know I have died before. Somehow, I know what it's like to experience that moment of exquisite anguish, sadness and fear, and then it just goes. I find that hugely comforting.

I was very struck by Katherine's description of what she believes death will be like. This leads us into the next chapter, which explores the extraordinary transition from life into death. However, because so many of us are unaware about what happens when someone starts to die, this chapter also outlines the physical and psychological processes that lead up to death.

CHAPTER 11

THE TRANSITION

~

I believe we all possess a kind of transpersonal life-clock which ticks happily away until it senses that time in our physical body is running out. Then a profound change takes place. For some, our life-clock ticks for decades. For others, it can stop ticking at birth or even before birth. Some people's life-clock stops suddenly or violently while other life-clocks wind down slowly. In some cases, a person passes through life so quickly that it's as if they've just dropped by to show us what unconditional love and compassion are really all about.

I believe that deep down we know when we are going to die. Many dying people certainly know their time is up, and I have heard countless stories of people feeling compelled to complete a project, or sort out their finances, or get in touch with people they haven't seen for years, only to die a short time after.

I will never forget meeting a mother from Washington State in the US whose seventeen-year-old son had been killed in a hiking accident. Several weeks after his death, she found a picture under his bed, which she showed me. Her son had drawn himself lying at the foot of a crevasse with a broken leg, jagged red and yellow colours streaking out from the break. This is exactly how he had died. My feisty friend Sarah also knew she wouldn't be around for long. It was well before her Parkinson's diagnosis.

Fiona is her early sixties. A few years ago, her husband died in a freak drowning accident in the sea. She remains convinced that he knew unconsciously that he was going to die.

> It was the weirdest thing, but when I looked back on what happened, it became clear to me that my husband somehow knew he was going to die even though he was fit and well and only in his fifties. Four or five weeks before his accident he put everything in place as if he was finishing things off. He went to see everyone who was important to him, whom he hadn't seen for a while. He took his son on a special weekend trip, which he particularly made time for. He wrote down a recipe for his favourite veggie pie, taking photos of every stage of the preparation. He chucked out things he no longer wanted and, while doing this, he

indicated to a box. This, he said to me, was 'all the archive material.' It was the way he looked at me, as if I was going to become responsible for it. He also told me that he loved me during the week before he died. I am sure he was trying to stay alive when he fell in the water, but it was very strange how things seem to conspire against rescuing him. The tide turned and started to pull him out and the rescue boat was on another emergency call. Other boats did finally arrive, but he'd been face down in the water for three minutes by then. However awful it is to lose him I just feel it was his time.

A friend recently told me how someone she knows well said to her that he 'has seen and done everything he wants to.' My friend said there was such a sense of acceptance and finality about how he said this that she realised that in his own way, he was preparing her for his death. My friend said she had to bite down on the urge to say, 'Don't say that. You've got years ahead to enjoy.' Instead she understands that what he was saying needs to be respected, however hard it is to hear.

On the other hand, someone in their late seventies, who came to a Death Café, wanted to know when she was doing to die. 'It would be such a relief. I could make my end of life plans, prepare my children and grandchildren and then get on with the life I have left without fear of the unknown hanging over me. If only life was as simple as that.' Indeed, if only life could be that simple.

Things start to happen

Placing sudden death aside, when time begins to run out, something starts to change. I saw this with both of my parents and have heard many stories from people who have witnessed relatives and friends enter their dying process. Virtually everyone talks about becoming aware of a tipping point that occurs when the person stops being 'ill' and starts to let go. This letting go may take months, but something alters in their psyche and they begin to relate to life differently. For instance, some may change their language and start talking about 'going home' in some way. Some, as I've already mentioned, feel pressed to put their finances in order, to make a will, or to settle old grievances. Some become more frightened of what lies ahead. Some, particularly parents of small children, start fighting for all they're worth to stay alive. Others develop a spiritual curiosity and may start asking questions or reading books about religious or spiritual beliefs. Others, again, develop a serenity that hasn't been present before.

However, because we are not educated to recognise when the dying process is starting, or we are too afraid of confronting it either due to our own fear of death or our fear of upsetting the dying person, we often pretend it isn't happening. Therefore, death becomes the elephant in the room.

Opening up the conversation

Having said that, it is essential to be sensitive to the needs of the dying person. Some people prefer to remain ignorant of what's happening, and this has to be respected. One interviewee said that she did everything she could to help her father to open up a conversation about what was happening, but he constantly refused. 'In the end I had to accept he was never going to talk. He wasn't ready to go, and I felt it wasn't up to me to push it any further.'

Yet denial leaves family and friends holding this uncomfortable truth with nowhere to go with it. Clare has five siblings and candidly speaks about how she and her sisters constantly colluded in denial around her ninety-one-year-old mother's impending death – until Clare pierced the bubble.

My mother has always been very controlling and is adamant she 'isn't going to die.' However, we have a disabled sister who lives with her, so I knew something had to be said – things will need to be sorted out. But when Mum began to feel ill, the doctor only alluded to the fact she was probably beginning to die. He told her, 'Do what you want to do – don't do anything you don't want to do.' I found this difficult. It's so obvious she doesn't have that long left and I found not being able to name this with my siblings completely counterintuitive. So, I did. I told my disabled sister that mum was going to die. This set off a whole chain reaction between me and my siblings, which has been both challenging and revealing. But I couldn't go on with the denial anymore. It felt as if I was holding a fantasy in my hand. The situation had become so stressful and tense between us; it was as if we were all stepping around each other on broken glass.

I feel I can breathe again, and it's broken a spell around my mother – we can all see how much she has manipulated us into obeying her our entire lives. Naming she's going to die has released the dread of her death turning into a nightmare, full of dramas into believing it is now possible for her death to be peaceful, beautiful and gentle, and we as siblings can join together to consciously help this happen.

Clare's story illustrates the importance of finding ways to unburden ourselves of the distress that the denial of death creates. As in Clare's case, this may be about having the courage to talk to other family members, or it may mean finding someone outside the family unit to talk things through with. It is equally important to set up support for children of dying parents.

On the other hand, relatives and friends may choose to be in denial of what's staring them in the face. This can be incredibly difficult for the dying person who wants a frank, open talk but realises this is too painful for those they love. There is a lot to be said for the old-fashioned parish priest's paying visits to the ill and the dying. Important private conversations can take place, and relatives can be supported to face the truth, so the end of life is eased for everyone involved.

Marianne told me a very touching story about how she plucked up the courage to ask her dying father what had been the most amazing thing about his life. The whole family was around his bed, including her mother; they had been married for sixty years.

> Without a beat, he looked across at mum, and said, 'Your mother.' It took us completely by surprise. Dad had been a highly successful businessman and had achieved all sorts of amazing things, but, on his deathbed, his love for Mum was the only thing that mattered. I realised they cared for each other, but I had no idea about his depth of love for her. It was such a beautiful thing to hear, and it made me feel really special, too.

Spiritual respect

It's essential not to put our own religious or spiritual beliefs onto the dying person. They need the time and space to work out what's right for them, even if this means they struggle with what faith means

– or, indeed, they have no belief in anything – right until the end.

It's also important to understand that the dying choose whom they want to talk to. It may not be their spouse, or children, or friends. It may not be their doctor, either, or any medical professional, come to that. Rather, they may feel safer talking to the hospital volunteer who brings them a cup of tea, or to a junior nurse, or even a stranger whom they bump into the pub, on a train, or in a bus. This is why I believe that Death Cafés are so important. They provide a safe, confidential space for people, whether they are dying or not, to talk together about what really matters.

Having said that, the death of a parent, especially the second one, can bring up all manner of family feuds and unresolved issues. It is not usual for family relationships to fracture completely. But the death of parents can also bring estranged siblings together again. Meeting death is an intense time for everyone, and it often needs patience and understanding, and a willingness to communicate openly and truthfully.

Spiritual midwives or death doulas are doing a lot of good work in this area. A doula was originally a non-medical person who acts as a birth companion and post-birth supporter to a woman before she gives birth and during labour. The name death doula[51] has now been attributed to non-medical people who are trained to help and support the dying and their families in the last few weeks of life. Even though they are making inroads, the great majority of people (again, mainly in Western cultures) remain ignorant of what actually happens when someone approaches the end of life.

The majority of hits that I receive on my website are linked to what happens physically when we die. Therefore, this next section looks at what takes place during the initial stages of dying and during our actual dying experience. It is a generic description, which cannot relate to everyone's dying process, but readers who have sat with the dying will recognise some of it, if not most of it. Many of the following signs are also described in the booklet, *Nearing the End of Life: a guide for relatives, friends and carers.*[52]

Our world shrinks

When death starts to call to us, our external world begins to diminish. We tend to lose interest in what's going on around us, and often lose interest in close relationships as well. This is hardly surprising because, as our body closes down, it becomes an effort to engage physically with conversations that are no longer important to us. This can be very upsetting for relatives and friends, but it is a natural process of letting go of this physical world.

Eventually, we prefer to stay at home, or our health diminishes to the extent that we become hospitalised or admitted into a care home or stabilised in a hospice. It's important to understand that this is a preparation time for us to ready ourselves for a different state of being.

We lose the strength or will to talk

As we become increasingly immobile, we often find it too tiring to talk for any length of time and spend a lot of time asleep or dozing. Again, this can be distressing for those who love us, but it's important to understand that any physical exertion at this stage is exhausting. As we deepen into our dying process, we may drift into semi-consciousness or become completely unconscious. I believe that during this stage we are living into two worlds – our physical world and the world that is opening up to us. But we need time to adjust to the energy of this new 'world' before we are ready to take the ultimate step.

We lose the desire to eat

As our systems close down, we naturally lose the desire to eat. Our body knows it no longer needs food to keep going, so we lose weight, often rapidly. This can cause further distress for relatives and friends who instinctively want to tempt us with anything to get us to eat or drink. But, it's important not to force food or drink when it's not wanted. It's much better and kinder to give gentle mouth care and offer regular sips of water or thin soup when requested.

Physical changes

Our skin can become paper-thin and pale, with dark liver spots appearing on our hands, feet and face. Our hair can also thin dramatically, and as our skeletal frame begins to shrink, we diminish in size. Our teeth, also, often discolour or develop dark stains. This is a completely normal part of the dying process, caused by our body systems closing down and getting ready to release us into what comes next.

Change of language

As I mentioned earlier, we often change our language, or use language we have never spoken before. For example, we may feel compelled to talk about 'leaving', 'flying', 'going home', 'being taken home', 'being collected', 'going on holiday' or making some kind of journey. We may also feel that we want to express heart-felt gratitude to those who are caring for us as part of saying our farewells. Some of us experience deathbed visions.

Deathbed visions

There are numerous reports of the dying talking about seeing dead friends or relatives – even pets – who have arrived to 'take them away'[53].' The dying will often say something along the lines of, 'Mary is here to collect me' (a wife who died several years before). One workshop participant said that her dying mother kept saying that her sister was in the next room, making petticoats while she waited for her! Some speak about hearing or seeing children who appear to be singing to them and are greatly comforted by them. Others at the point to death may look up and die with a huge smile on their face – as if someone much loved has come to collect them.

This doesn't always happen, but it's important for carers to pay attention when it does. This is part of creating wholeness at the end of life. Noticing changes in language or behaviour can often initiate profound healing conversations, which help to ease the grief of relatives.

Special requests

When we know that life is coming to an end, we may feel a pressing need to do something special such as to visit a particular site, or be surrounded by our favourite flowers, or to hear certain music. We may feel compelled to go through family photographs or photographs of our childhood, or to make contact with someone who has been important in our life. This helps us to make peace with our life and put it into context.

Death takes its own time

It's impossible to predict the actual moment of death. Dying takes its own time, and this can be emotionally gruelling for those who sit with us. I can remember supporting a friend whose partner was in the final stages of AIDS. After days of being constantly at his bedside, my friend asked me, almost in despair, 'When *is* he going to die?'

It really can feel like that. And, it's perfectly natural, so try not to feel guilty if this happens to you. It's not a lot of fun to sit beside someone who's in pain and distress. Just remember: even though it may seem as if death is *never* going to come, it certainly will. And when it does it can be so quick that it's easy to miss the final moment.

So here are certain signs, which indicate when death is fairly imminent. We may not experience all these indicators as we die, but we will experience some of them.

Congestion in our lungs

Our breath becomes shallow and laboured, and it can sound as if we are gurgling. This can be alarming for those caring for us. However, it's quite normal. It's caused by our swallow reflex diminishing and secretions pooling in the back of our throat.

Yawning

Even when we are in a semi-conscious or unconscious state, we may often yawn. This is a natural reflex to draw more oxygen into our body. Our systems haven't as yet completely shut down.

Coldness in our extremities

Our hands, arms, feet and legs become icy cold, caused by our blood circulation closing down. This changes our skin colour to almost white.

Tea-coloured urine

This is caused by the lack of fluid intake and our kidneys ceasing to function. It makes our urine concentrated and tea-coloured, which produces a pungent acetone smell that can pervade the room. Dying and death has a distinct smell that often takes people by surprise.

Incontinence

This, again, is a natural part of our dying experience. As our body systems cease to operate, we lose muscle control over our bladder and bowel. When we are completely bedbound, this may involve lying on pads, or, in some cases, nurses may insert a catheter into our bladder. I would imagine by now that many of us are so far into our dying process that being incontinent is not a major concern. I certainly hope so.

Agitation and restlessness

Some of us may become confused and agitated about what feels real: especially those of us with dementia. We may be dipping in and out of our past experiences, calling out people's names who have long been dead, or we may cry out in alarm at the changes that we are experiencing in our body and mind. Or we may be half living in the world that is to come only to find ourselves back in our increasingly toxic dying body again. I imagine this dipping in and out may feel be strange and stressful. Medical staff often administer medication to calm us down.

Dark bruising

As our heart loses its ability to pump oxygen around the body, our blood begins to coagulate, or pool, particularly at the base of our spine. This drains the skin of colour and creates patches, which look like dark purple bruising.

Smell

As I have already mentioned, death does have a certain smell, which is not very pleasant. It's caused by our body systems closing down, which create a distinctive acetone odour. Having said this, while nursing a dying patient, I experienced the room filling with the most beautiful aroma immediately on her death. This person was a truly good soul and it felt as if she had been received into the world beyond in joy and celebration.

We no longer respond

We have reached very near the end now. We are no longer able to communicate even when awake. We may be taking rasping breath through an open mouth, which sounds as if we're snoring. This can make our mouths dry, so it's soothing to receive gentle mouth washes.

Our breathing pattern changes

This happens to many people as they die. Their breathing starts to alternate between loud rasping breaths to periodic breathing called Cheyne-Stokes breathing – a cycle of taking an in-breath followed by no breath for several seconds. This can sound very alarming and confusing for those at the bedside who believe the person has died, only for breathing to start again. I remember sitting with my father for hours listening to his Cheyne-Stokes breathing. Each time he stopped breathing I tensed in anticipation that this would be his last, only for him to take another rasping breath. It became exhausting.

When it happens, it happens quickly

The actual moment of death is remarkably quick, lasting a few seconds, if that. The person may suddenly give a couple of outward pants as their heart and lungs cease to function. Or they may give one long out-breath and then they are gone. Some people just quietly stop breathing. But this time, there is no doubt that it's taken place. There's no longer a pulse. Their skin colour drains to a sallow pale yellow. Their facial expression changes or loosens as their personality disappears, to the extent that some people find it hard to recognise them. Whoever they were has gone. There is literally no one home anymore. Yet, this is when an extraordinary sense of peace may settle onto what used to be their face.

Deathbed coincidences

A remarkable thing can take place at the moment of death. An end-of-life experience study reports that of those interviewed, 90% of people who were nowhere near the dying person, and sometimes lived on the opposite side of the world, experienced a 'visit' from the dead person.[54] These mostly comforting visits inform the person of their death and there's a feeling that the dead person is saying farewell.

44% said they did not know, at the time, that the person had died, which was only confirmed later through, for example, a phone call. Many reported that the moment they 'saw' the dead person was the precise moment they had physically died. These deathbed coincidences add to mounting evidence that some form of consciousness continues after death.

Love calls us home

Thomas Keating, priest of the Cistercian order, and author of countless books on centreing prayer, said that the dying process is the culmination or the peak of the whole development of the spiritual journey.

I agree with him. I have sat with a number of people as they die, and, to me, something profound happens as they enter the liminal space of the dying process. It feels to me as if the veil between the seen world and unseen world suddenly thins to give us a glimpse of what the Love of the Universe is all about.

It reminds me that love is embedded inside all of us. Everything in our life is coloured by it, whether we are desperately searching for it (look at the explosion of Internet dating sites) or we are lucky enough to find it through a relationship, a close friendship, through the love of a child or grandchild, or we find love through a career or hobby that completely fulfils us. I believe that our death is the moment when we are reunited with this greater Love. So, in a way, while we are just passing through our physical existence, each one of us is an ambassador for Universal Love. We forget, that's all. Even people who have difficult deaths, or fight death to the very end, often seem to find a sense of peace at the moment they die – as I witnessed with my mother.

Yes, I've heard of deaths devoid of love, which cause great distress when they happen. Carrie, who is in her late forties, told me how her father fought against death right until the end. She also told me that he refused to talk about his death, and she had no idea if he had a faith. She, herself, believes that death is the end. Nothing exists after.

> There was no comfort. I found it horrendous. He looked terrified. It makes me furious when people bang on about dying well or having wonderful deaths. It didn't happen to my dad. It was so awful I wish I hadn't been there. But I have made myself forget what happened. I just focus on thinking about him when he was alive. He was such a lovely, generous, kind person. I loved him so much.

To me, Carrie's willingness to be with her father in such distress is all about greater love. What more can do we for someone we love as much as this? Death cuts through all the bullshit.

Love the transformer

I never cease to be moved by the role that love can play in the dying process. Jo, a journalist in her fifties, told me about the transformative process of love while sitting with her dying mother.

> Although I got on well with my mother, it had been a difficult and emotionally challenging relationship for me throughout my life. When she was ill in hospital, all the pain and sadness from those experiences lifted and I felt I met her at a soul level. I was at her bedside at the end of her life and it was an extraordinary healing time. I hope I was able to help her go 'home', understanding that she and I had both been teachers for one another. I understood at a profound level what LOVE is. Words alone cannot explain the depth and purity of that experience save to say it transcended my earthly understanding of the word love.

Love gives us the strength to hold liminal space for the dying person, even when we really don't like them, or they have caused us great suffering. Barbara is in her early sixties. Her father was very abusive during her childhood, to the extent that she ran away from home in her mid-teens. She rarely saw him but felt the need to visit him when she heard that he was dying.

There was something about seeing him lying in the bed that cracked open something in my heart. He had been awful to me. Simply awful. I suffered throughout my life because of what he did. But I suddenly saw him as this vulnerable old dying man and something changed. I wept and wept, not because he was dying, but because of both our brokenness. Even at the end when he turned his face away rather than look at me, it didn't matter anymore. I was relieved that he was going to be finally released from the torment he was in. It released me too. I still struggle with mental health issues, but the sting has gone. I am much more conscious of my path in life and this helps me to find peace with who I am.

Love helps us to die

I believe the presence of love helps us to die. I witnessed this with my eighty-eight-year-old father after a massive stroke destroyed half his brain, leaving him semi-conscious, completely paralysed down one side and unable to speak. Only the week before, he had told me how terrified he was of going into 'an old people's home.' He also told me that he did not want to be resuscitated if anything happened to him.

'I want to die like my mother,' he said. His mother, robust in health well into her eighties, dropped down in the street one day as she walked home with her shopping. She was dead within the week. That is exactly what happened to my father.

Following his hospital admission, I agreed with medical staff to stop life extending treatments and place him on an end-of-life care plan. My father was put into a side ward with large windows that overlooked the same playing fields where he had cheered on numerous schoolboys playing rugby and cricket throughout his long career as a schoolmaster. I, too, knew these playing fields well, and the sight of them soothed me as I sat beside him for seven days while he took his time to die.

During this time, and even though he was more or less unconscious and incapable of communicating, I was convinced that he had entered a space where he was being somehow taught to let go. I can't explain why I felt this, but I did. It seemed as if he was listening to something deep inside. There was nothing fearful about it, and he certainly wasn't agitated. He would then sleep, semi wake up again, and continue to listen. I found this profoundly moving as the days progressed. I was also very curious about the way he would reach out with his good hand to grasp hold of some substance I couldn't see. He would rub it between his fingers as if trying to work out what it was. Again, there was no fear attached to this, just curiosity. This certainly wasn't a drug-induced hallucination (he wasn't on any medication) or when agitated people 'pluck' at the air during their last days.

I also felt compelled to arrange for a priest to give him the last rites on the day before he died.

This was another deeply moving and heart opening experience for me as I watched the priest draw the sign of the cross on my father's forehead. I arrived back at his bedside the following morning, a few moments before he took his last breaths, and was able to throw open the window and say to him 'Fly Dad, Fly'. I have never forgotten that or how rapidly his life force vacated his body.

The space, which he and I created together in those last few days of his life, was transformative for both of us. While he was being 'educated' I realised there was no practical information for relatives and friends to understand what was happening when someone dies, which inspired Dr Peter Fenwick and me to co-author our booklet, *Nearing the End of Life; a guide for relatives, friends and carers.* So, my father's transition through liminal space, and the love that I experienced while sitting with him, became a highly creative space for me.

I asked Peter Fenwick to explain what happens during our transition into death. Peter is a neuropsychiatrist, and a member of the Royal Society of Medicine, who has held many prestigious positions during his long career. I was fortunate to be Peter's honorary researcher for a five-year retrospective study into end-of-life experiences where we explored what happens to the dying during their final months, weeks, days and moments of death. Peter has also co-authored several books with his wonderful wife, Elizabeth, including, *The Art of Dying.*

When you start to die you enter into a transition that has three parts to it. First, your ego loosens. You become less fixed in your old persona. There's an increasingly strong recognition that you are well under way. Second, there's a sense of passing through into another state of being. Third, (this is usually during the final week of life) you start to relinquish any sense of self and the ego and move into a far more cosmic or transcendent state, where consciousness expands into Love and light. This final stage is the moment when the dying often realise they have never been born, and they will never die. They are part of consciousness, and they have always been part of it. I am put in mind of what Buddha said when he saw the morning star on the horizon: 'Before you, I was.' Dying consciously has that transcendent quality to it. People often ask me to define consciousness. I can't. It's impossible to define. I refer to it as the totality of the Universe.

We die in three ways: Suddenly through accidents, suicide and violent events, consciously preparing for death, or with terminal anxiety. There's not a lot you can do about preparing for sudden death, apart from making sure you always have your affairs in order. To die consciously you have to have done a whole lot of work on yourself and your relationships. You need to understand and accept that death is inevitable, and that life continues in some form after death. We all have to face ourselves on our deathbed. Don't leave it until you are dying. Face yourself while you live so you can do something about it and break through into your own transcendence and illumination.

When you are too afraid to engage with your mortality, you can't face the fact that you are going to die. This denial and fear makes you increasingly upset and agitated as death nears. You lose your capacity of how you used to be. Your mind doesn't work like it used to, so you are no longer able to connect with things that gave you reassurance. This is a terrifying place to find yourself in. But this is not how it needs to be. Everyone can choose to die consciously. The skill is to develop a curiosity about what is coming, and to develop a positive attitude. Research shows that regular meditation, prayer and other types of spiritual practice help you to engage with your death.

Personally, I want to die quietly. I want to have reached a point where I just give everything up – that I transcend and ascend within and recognise that the inner Light has always been with me, and always will be. I will return to who I am as part of everything. So, for me, there is no question about being alone when I die. I believe that all the cleansing and clearing that happens at

the point of death will allow to me to release
my ego and become back to the Light. And,
yes, I would love to think that Elizabeth, my
wife, will be there, holding my hand.

This beautiful description of what death may be
like leads us on to the fascinating question of what
happens in our brain as we die.

CHAPTER 12

LIFE AFTER DEATH

Recently I was invited by Peter Fenwick to present a paper at the Royal Society of Medicine on the liminal space and dying process. Preparing the paper led me to explore some extraordinary scientific research of what may happen to consciousness in the dying brain. There are no absolute answers but there are some pointers.

Francis Crick (he died in 2004) and Christof Koch pioneered research into where the heart of consciousness may reside in the brain[55]. They suggested an area of the brain called the claustrum. The claustrum is a sheet of cells situated deep in the centre of the brain, which may bind together the constant flow of perceptions and information that we receive from different parts of our brain networks. In other words, the claustrum could act similarly to an orchestral leader in conducting all these different perceptions and information into a cohesive whole.

Why is this important to consider? Well, it seems increasingly evident that consciousness does not die or end at the same time as clinical death takes place.

Death and deep sleep

There's an intriguing study published in the *Canadian Journal of Neurological Sciences* into the brain activity of four terminally ill dying people.[56] When their life support was turned off, one of them showed persistent brain activity for a further ten minutes, even after being declared clinically dead, including the absence of a pulse and nonreactive pupils.

The patient appeared to experience the same kind of brain waves that we have during deep sleep. Deep sleep is called delta, or slow wave sleep, where people are far less responsive and less aware of their external environment than in other states of sleep. But the delta sleep state may also be important in helping to clear the brain for new learning and reducing the production of Cortisol - a stress hormone.[57]

The fact that one patient's brain activity was still present in a deep sleep state after clinical death prompted me to wonder whether the claustrum remains active while these brain waves, in some form, are present. And, perhaps, this deep sleep state is being orchestrated by the claustrum to help the dead person to reduce stress and clear the way for new learning so he or she can accept that death has occurred.

I am no neuroscientist so I don't know, but my speculation has made me ask a lot of questions about the role of liminal space during the dying process and what may be going on in the dying and clinically dead brain. This research could indicate that some people remain in a kind of conscious liminal state for several minutes after they have died while their brain makes sense of what is happening to them.

It also prompts me to wonder if, and why, some dying and dead people might need more time to cross over the threshold than others. Are these people more resistant to death, and therefore less willing to let go? Do they require more time for their claustrum (if this is indeed, the seat of consciousness) to orchestrate their conscious perceptions together in delta wave state to accept that they have died? Or are they merely adjusting to their own natural rhythms of consciousness and acceptance while they transition from one state of being to another?

This particular study on the dying brain can't address my questions because it focused on what happens in the dying and clinically dead brain rather than the emotional or spiritual state of the dying person. But it's exciting how end-of-life researchers such as Dr Peter Fenwick and Dr Monica Renz, author of *Hope and Grace: Spiritual Experiences in Severe Distress, Illness and Dying,* are reporting the spiritual experiences of dying people. As I mentioned in the previous chapter, many patients appear to express joy at the moment of death or speak about much loved dead relatives coming to 'take them away', suggesting to me that consciousness does continue as we cross over the threshold.[58]

Furthermore, clinical studies into near-death experiences (NDEs) brought about by cardiac arrest are adding scientific data to anecdotal accounts of what may happen to consciousness in the dying and dead brain.

The dying brains of rats

An extraordinary (if not disturbing) study has been conducted on the dying brains of rats[59] as part of an on-going clinical study into what happens to the brain of someone experiencing an NDE during a cardiac arrest. Led by Jimo Borjigin, associate professor of molecular and integrative physiology at the University of Michigan Medical School, the study shows that within the first thirty seconds following an induced cardiac arrest, the rats displayed highly aroused brain activity. The data postulates that the mammalian brain (rats, of course, are mammals) has the potential for high levels of internal information processing during clinical death. And since we, too, are mammals, this information processing may be happening to us as we die. The research proposes that these findings will form the foundation for future investigation into what may happen in the human dying brain during a cardiac arrest.

Currently, they report that approximately 20% of human cardiac arrest survivors in their study experience NDE during clinical death. Some of these survivors described, for example, floating above their body and watching doctors administer life-saving treatments. They were able to describe what was happening to them and to repeat conversations that took place around their bed as they were being resuscitated.

Largest NDE study to date

The largest and most rigorous study into NDEs is led by Dr Sam Parnia who is director of the Human Consciousness Project at the University of Southampton.[60] The study involved 2060 cardiac arrest patients in the UK, America and Australia. Of that number, 330 survived and 40% of those survivors reported being partly aware during the time that they were 'clinically dead' and before they were resuscitated. One in five said they had felt an unusual sense of peacefulness. A third reported that time had slowed down or speeded up. Some recalled seeing a bright light, such as a golden flash or the sun shining. Others spoke about feelings of fear or drowning or being dragged through deep water. 13% said they had felt separated from their bodies and a further 13% said their senses had been heightened. From these results, Parnia suggests that during the first few minutes after death, consciousness is not annihilated. However, it remains unknown whether it remains or fades away afterwards.

In an interview with the Telegraph,[61] Parnia outlines how his multi-disciplined research team wanted to "go beyond the emotionally charged yet poorly defined term of 'near-death experiences' to explore objectively what happens when we die". He states that while it is not possible to prove patients' experiences or claims of awareness (only 2% of patients in his study explicitly recalled visual awareness or out of body experiences), it was impossible to disclaim them either. He concluded that much more study needs to be done into consciousness and the dying brain. I find this very exciting.

NDE traits

Rigorous scientific study is one avenue for gathering evidence for NDEs. However, there are hundreds of books written by ordinary people who say they have experienced NDEs. Dr Raymond Moody was the first person to use the term 'near-death experience' in his best-selling book, *Life After Life*. He collected thousands of stories from people from all walks of life who described certain NDE traits. For example, some spoke of seeing pure white light. Some described having an out-of-body experience (as described by resuscitated cardiac patients). Others spoke about entering another realm or dimension, which can be welcoming or, in some cases, frightening. Some spoke about encountering angels or a benevolent presence or even God.

Many seemed to find themselves travelling down a tunnel of light where they were met by benevolent beings or much loved dead relatives. They were usually informed that this 'isn't your time,' and they (usually reluctantly) found themselves back in their body again. Some spoke of undergoing a life review, where their entire life flashed in front of them, and they returned to life pressed to do things differently (this is certainly what happened to me during a mystical experience, which we will come to a little later on).

The common factors in the vast majority of NDE accounts is that life is never the same again and the person loses their fear of death

Personal NDE stories

I have read countless books on NDEs. Even though each story of how the person 'died' due to an accident or illness and then came back to life might be remarkably different, almost every account of the hereafter is the same: there's a sublime, loving and peaceful place waiting to welcome them home. The experience gives them a profound understanding of what it feels like to be part of an all-expanded loving consciousness. They describe what happens as so exquisite that they don't want to return to life, but they know they have some task to accomplish, which usually involves telling their story to help other people to release their fear of death. Some, such as Dr Alan Hugenot, an American semi-retired naval architect and marine engineer, speak about developing psychic and mediumship skills following an NDE[62]. I am moved by Alan Hugenot's story because it's courageous for a scientist not just to admit to possessing psychic skills, but to use them to help others as well.

This certainly happened to American neurosurgeon Dr Eben Alexander, too. Formerly a highly cynical, hardwired neuroscientist, he portrays vividly, in his best-selling book *Proof of Heaven,* how he fell into a coma from which he wasn't expected to survive. During the time he remained in the coma, he had an NDE, which changed his entire life. He is now an international speaker on NDEs and how he has integrated his own NDE experience to help people feel less fearful of death.[63]

Neuroanatomist Jill Bolte Taylor also provides an extraordinary account in her book, *My Stroke of Insight*, of what happened when the left logical side of her brain was damaged after she suffered a stroke. She describes how her creative and intuitive right brain took over and she felt as if she merged with the beauty and love of Universal consciousness itself. Her account of her right brain experience has many similarities to how Eben Alexander describes his NDE.

So, again, I am going to speculate. Could this mean that as we prepare to leave our body, the left logical side of our brain tones down and allows the right creative side of our brain to merge into this all-inclusive consciousness – and the liminal space of the dying process is where this cross over happens?

I don't know. But I love thinking about it. Whatever, there are too many similar NDE narratives for me to retain even a modicum of scepticism about the existence of life after death. Then again, I have had some strange experiences myself.

Mystical Experiences

I haven't had an NDE, but I had a profound mystical experience, which convinced me that death is merely the threshold to a completely different level of consciousness.

My mystical experience happened in the most ordinary of settings, several years after the plane crash. It was mid-morning on a lovely sunny summer's day. I was seated beside a grimy window, travelling at speed in a nondescript carriage of a south-coast Inter-city train, opposite a woman who was reading a newspaper. I turned to watch green fields flash by when suddenly the 'curtains' between my eyebrows parted and everything dissolved. I found myself floating upwards into dark sparkling light. Even though I no longer had a body, I was still very much 'me', but without the angst. I became aware of a pure loving acceptance that I had never experience before – it felt as if I was part of it, and it was part of me. Any sense of separation dissolved. I noticed that this loving acceptance was tinged (if that's the right word) with quiet, gentle humour. I felt such an incredible feeling of peace that anything troubling me just melted away. I then became aware of a benevolent presence – a kind of telepathic benevolent presence – surrounding me. There was no sense of judgement or criticism. It simply seemed to know me and love me. I wanted to stay with this presence forever.

Something prompted me to look down at my left-hand side. I saw a lion-yellow colour streaming out of my body around hip height. Instinctively I knew that this stream of colour held my life story and I could dive into it and explore anything I wanted to. I also knew I was aged seventy-six and, for some reason, I was being shown that a life review was going to happen when I finally leave my physical body – which I assume is when I reach seventy-six.

Then I heard the presence (or telepathic communication) say in the gentlest way, 'Life is just an experience. That's all it is.'

Immediately I thought, 'Oh, yes, of course it is. Life really *is* only that.' I wanted to ask the presence more, but the curtains between my eyes abruptly closed, and I was back on the train again. I couldn't believe what had just happened. The countryside was still whizzing past on the other side of the grimy window. The woman opposite was still reading her paper. But I was overcome with grief, completely bereft of the love that I had experienced.

I mourned the loss of this love for months afterward. Even now, writing about it well over two and a half decades later brings back the memory of it. But I can't touch it like I did then, and that triggers grief again. But I know that what I experienced and felt is where I come from and where I will return to when my time in this physical body is done.

I often imagine that C.S. Lewis had a mystical experience, which inspired him to write the *The Lion, The Witch, and the Wardrobe*. Once you've been to Narnia you yearn to go back. It's the same for me. I have prayed, begged and pleaded for the curtains between my eyebrows to open again. They never have.

However, I had another very strange experience during my first night on Jem Bendell's Deep Adaptation retreat in a retreat centre hidden away in the Yorkshire Dales. I met my roommate, a delightful Canadian poet with a flowing mane of red hair, shortly before we turned in early for the night in preparation for the next three days. We knew it was going to be fraught because deep adaptation considers the emotional and spiritual implications of it being too late to avert climate catastrophe.[64]

It must have been around 2:00 a.m. when I found myself awake, but, at the same time, as if I was in a dream state. I felt a tall benevolent presence standing beside my bed, who calmly pulled my covers over me and lovingly tucked me up as if I was a child. The presence blew gently on my cheek and I fell back to sleep.

In the morning, the vision of what had happened was so vivid that I asked my roommate if she had pulled the covers over me, tucked me up and blown on my cheek. She looked at me in alarm. 'No!' she said.

Feeling slightly disturbed, I went outside to join, for breakfast, three other participants whom I had met fleetingly the evening before. I told them about the presence beside my bed, expecting them to confirm that it had been a dream. At the end of the table an older woman with long straight brown hair conveying a quiet, steady demeanour, stared at me in amazement. 'That's exactly what happened to me,' she said, a mixture of surprise and incredulity spreading across her face. 'I woke up in the early hours to find a loving presence beside my bed, who pulled the covers over me, tucked me up as if I was a child and then stretched out their hands to give me healing over my stomach area. When they finished, I went straight to back to sleep. If you hadn't mentioned it, I would have dismissed it as a dream.'

I learnt that her name was Pam. She had never had an experience like this before either. Nor is she given to flights of fancy. Pam is a very grounded, successful CEO of an organisation, based in Scotland, which works with sustainability and resilience. This, to me, made the whole experience even more extraordinary.

Together we told the retreat centre owner what had happened. She shrugged her shoulders and said that nothing like this had been reported before, although she did tell us about a friendly ghost who lived in her house down the hill. Pam and I *knew* that our loving visitor hadn't been a ghost. It had unquestionably been an angel.

Obviously, on hearing our story, everyone on the retreat wanted the angel to tuck them up, too. But it never appeared again. Writing about this, now, makes me wonder why it appeared to only Pam and me rather than anyone else. But life is full of mysteries like this. Having been very skeptical about the existence of angels, I have certainly changed my mind.

Mystical experiences are common

There are thousands of accounts of mystical experiences reported throughout the ages by famous mystics as well as so called ordinary people. These are not usual occurrences, but many go unreported by 'ordinary people' who are afraid of being dismissed or ridiculed or told it can't have happened because they are not religious. I'm not either, but my mystical experience certainly happened to me, and my angel was very real to me to the point that the encounter completely changed my attitude towards angels. Previously, I thought they were flights of fancy. If you want to read more about mystic experiences, I highly recommend Marianne Rankin's book, *Religious & Spiritual Experiences.*

I am ending this chapter with an interview with my friend Penny Satori, whose PhD research into NDEs has helped so many people to talk about their own 'strange' experiences. Penny is the best-selling author of *The Wisdom of Near-Death Experiences: how understanding NDEs can help us to live more fully.* When the book was serialised in a national paper, it received 300 comments by 10.00 am. 1200 responses had been posted by the evening. The newspaper continued to run extracts from the book for a further five days. She was then inundated with requests for interviews on radio and television and speaking engagements, to the point where her publisher had to step in to create an appointments diary. Within six months, Penny personally received 14000 emails from people from around the world. The book has now been translated into thirteen languages.

My book is the result of eight years of research that I did for my doctorate. It was an extraordinary time. I felt as if I had entered some kind of flow – everything seemed to slot into place – even obtaining funding so I could continue to research and write. Everything felt so abundant and prosperous.

I haven't personally had an NDE, but my fascination in death started when I had a strange encounter with a patient I was caring for. I suddenly experienced changing places with him. I felt the pain he was in, and then our eyes connected. It was as if he was saying, 'please let me die in peace.' At the time I was struggling with my job working as a nurse. I felt I had lost my way, and my soul was dying.

After this experience I suddenly realised that intensive care would be the perfect place to research the dying process and to help people make the transition in a better way. When I told my line manager I wanted to study near-death experiences, she laughed. However, I persevered and was accepted onto a PhD programme to study NDEs at Lampeter University. I am eternally grateful to Professor Paul Badham for helping to secure funding for the research.

The main message about NDEs is how people return to life a lot wiser than before they 'died.' We need to take notice of what they are telling us, because they have seen and experienced something that we haven't. They also realise how precious life is. So many of us forget this. We are just existing – there's no meaning to life. I believe this is reflected in the rise in mental health issues, especially depression.

There's no question that lots of people experience NDEs in hospital settings, but don't talk about them because they think medical staff will laugh or dismiss at them. Lots of very ill people are highly medicated too, so they are less likely to experience an NDE. But we can't dismiss this is happening any longer. Yet, when I talk to nurses, very few even think to ask a patient who has 'died' and come back if they have had NDE. One nurse said, 'It scared me.' This makes me angry. It's difficult to support people who have NDEs when medical staff are too afraid to engage with them. This is why I am so thrilled to be offered the post of Senior Lecturer in Adult Nursing at Swansea University – I hope I can make a difference.

We can learn so much from the NDEs about life and about death. How can we fear death if we know something wonderful is waiting for us? Personally, listening to so many stories about NDEs makes me think there's a Divine Plan that guides us. I have no idea what this is, but I have a deep knowing that it's there.

I want to die in a peaceful way and knowing I have lived life to the full and made a difference in the world. Nothing else matters, really.

If you have extraordinary experiences, don't be afraid to speak about them or write about them. Your story adds to growing scientific and anecdotal evidence that some form of life continues after death. The more we understand this, the more we release our fear of what happens when we die. Personally, I believe that releasing our fear of death is the next step in the evolution of human consciousness. When we accept that we come into human form for a finite time, we learn to cherish what it means to live and die.

I also believe this will become increasingly important as we begin to understand how the present changes and chaos we are experiencing across the globe are part of a much greater evolutionary shift for all life on Earth. In the final chapter, I outline how these changes have been foretold for eons. Realising how my life falls into a far bigger picture has helped me to engage much more profoundly with what living fully and dying consciously mean to me. Some of what I write about may be a stretch for some readers and jarring for others. Again, I have cited references so you can make up your own mind.

CHAPTER 13

WHY THIS MATTERS
SO MUCH

I don't think anyone can deny that we are living in times of great change. Global politics are in upheaval; international money markets move up and down like yoyos; anarchy (or more accurately people power) is on the rise and religions are polarising to protect their faith.

And, its heartbreaking to witness thousands of desperate migrants risking their lives to find a better way of being. Yet some people persist in saying the world has never experienced such an extended time of international peace. Try telling that to millions of refugees huddled in desolate makeshift camps located on borders of war-torn homelands.

What's more, this human-made chaos is propping itself up against the backdrop of both climate crisis and magnetic earth changes. I don't want to sound gloomy about the future. I believe we humans are fantastically creative when faced with a challenge, and, throughout the ages, our natural ability to adapt to our ever-fluctuating environment has ensured our survival. But something is most definitely UP.

It feels as if a perfect storm is brewing to offer us two alternatives at precisely the right time in this current moment of human evolution. Either we carry on with our hedonistic pursuits and take down the planet with us; or we join together to create a new way of being that will lift us collectively onto a higher level of consciousness. It is down to personal free-will choice. This is why developing spiritual wellbeing is so important, particularly at the present time. It stops us going mad in a world that *is* going mad.

Legends and prophecies

What gives me hope for the future of humanity and for all life on earth is that this time of unprecedented change has been foretold for millennia. For example, Buddha describes an apocalypse ending for our known world in his 'Sermon of the Seven Suns,' recorded in the Pali Canon said to date back to the first century BCE. But he also told of a golden time that would follow for those of his students who embraced his teachings of the Middle Way.

All three Abrahamic religions speak about a second coming of a major prophet, after a time of destruction, who will save the faithful.[65] My personal favourite is *The Book of Revelation*. It's not a very jolly read but for those of us into eschatology (the study of the end of things) the four riders of the apocalypse provide a wonderfully colourful epic drama of what is to come.

Many ancient prophecies also predict the end of the world. For example, the Hopi Indian prophecies[66] forecast an ending at some point, but, similar to Buddha's teachings, they also predict that some people will be 'saved,' while others will have to meet their fate.

Likewise, famous psychics such as Edgar Cayce and Delores Cannon predicted great changes for our modern world around this time. Delores Cannon focused on a major shift in human consciousness that would bring about a completely new earth.[67] She foresaw that many people, who no longer want to remain in the denser duality energies of separation and diversity, will collectively make a powerful spiritual or energetic (or quantum) leap, in our physical body, into a different dimensional frequency of non-duality and ultimate connectedness. Actually, I can see that a growing desire to end duality is happening for many of us. I am not so sure about physically jumping into a completely different dimensional reality. And, I'm also open to it.

Many people also believed that the end of the world would arrive when the Mayan calendar ran out in 2012.[68] It didn't do that, but I do see 2012 marking a time when our known, safe world began to draw to an end.

A change of cycle

The evolution of the world is also considered to be influenced by great cycles of existence. For example, Hindu Vedic texts, written between 1500 and 1000 BCE say that for the past twenty-six thousand years we have been travelling through an evolutionary cycle called the Kali Yuga.[69] The Kali Yuga – named after the Hindu goddess Kali who represents death, time, and doomsday – is said to have started in 3102 BCE and the final stage, or death throes, of the Kali Yuga will be felt acutely between 2019 and 2025, peaking in 2022. It certainly feels to me as if we are facing some kind of death throes at the moment.

But, again, there is hope. According to the Vedic texts, once humanity has moved through the Kali Yuga, we start a brand new twenty-six-thousand-year cycle in the Satya Yoga, also known as the Golden Age, where we experience what it's like to live in harmony and peace.

According to astrologers, we are also in the process of changing from the age of Pisces (I believe) into the age of Aquarius (I know), which means we are moving away from being told what to believe and how to believe it into a new energy of freedom, independence, rebellion, invention, and humanitarianism.[70] Extinction Rebellion, the environmental movement, which has risen up almost overnight to draw attention to global climate crisis, perfectly symbolises this new Aquarian energy.

Although no one knows quite when it started, some people say the shift from Pisces to Aquarius happened on 21st December 2012 when the Mayan calendar ran out. Others say we are right in the middle of a two hundred year cross over. At whatever stage we are in, both of these great changes of cycles are certainly manifesting in friction, tension and increased polarisation. People are either opening their hearts and minds to a new innovative energy or are fixated on maintaining the status quo.

Procession of the Equinoxes

These cyclical changes are not just prophecies and astrological hearsay. Called the procession of the Equinoxes, the Earth's electromagnet North Pole is currently moving at such a rate towards Russia that scientists constantly need to readjust satellite navigation systems and data to keep up with it.[71] An acceleration of this axis shift was recorded in 2004, which coincided with the Indonesian Tsunami.

Electromagnetic movement is not unusual. The earth's electromagnetic axis completes its cycle every 25,700 years. But it is poignantly synchronistic that this particular electromagnetic North Pole cycle is estimated to complete somewhere between 2020 and 2026 – which coincides with the predicted end of the Kali Yuga.

In 2015 the Innuits, who live in far northern areas of Alaska, Canada, Siberia and Greenland, reported to NASA that the earth had shifted, and this was the cause of climate change.[72] Leading scientists have now registered that due to the rate of this magnetic shift, the earth is currently wobbling on its axis and this is profoundly affecting our climate,[73] made worse by human disregard of the natural world.

I believe that the wobble is affecting us personally, too. At times, I have certainly been feeling an energetic wobble in my body. I have spoken to a number of people who are also experiencing this. One friend said that she keeps on finding herself walking to the right all the time! And, many people are talking about feeling exhausted, out of sorts, overwhelmed and believing they are ill when doctors fail to find anything wrong with them.

So, what can we do about it?

Environmental change is not *going* to happen. Environmental change *is* happening. The possibility of extinction has entered everyday conversations (currently between 10,000 and 100,000 species are becoming extinct each year). Jem Bendell's You Tube videos on Deep Adaptation[74] take a brave look at the realities of what we are all facing. In fact, British psychologists are now recognising a dramatic increase in climate crisis anxiety related issues.[75] Many fearful people are asking, 'What's the point if we only have a few years left to put things right?' It's a good question.

Humanity is certainly dealing with a new story minus a guaranteed fairy-tale ending. And, because of twenty-four-hour-a-day news exposure, climate anxiety is being continually burnt into our brain's neural networks, which means that people will begin to experience climate crisis related PTSD symptoms. Added to which, fears around artificial intelligence (AI) means that many of us can't see how we will fit into a future run by robots. What *will* our place be in world, let alone in the Universe?

It's understandable that when people are confronted by the enormity of what this could mean, they tend to stick their head so deep into the sand that they can see Australia. But it really doesn't help. Ignorance feeds fear. The first thing we have to do is to extract our head from the sand, then draw on our courage and reliance to look at our present-day challenges square in the eye. This is the only way to know what we are dealing with. A reality-check informs us of what kind of strategies we need to adopt to make the best of life on offer. Here are some suggestions:

Adopt a togetherness strategy

Okay, so individually we can't stop what's happening to our world – we may have gone beyond the tipping point now, but we can find ways to support each other in doing things better as our tenuous future unfolds. I believe this is when spiritual wellbeing truly comes into play. We are all in this together. So, let's start to find ways of productively working together. I am a great believer in the whole being far greater than the sum of its parts, which takes us back to the holon effect. For a start, wouldn't it be great if we all began to think in terms of how the Native American Indian Iroquois make decisions? Seemingly, any decision they make takes the next *seven* generations into consideration.[76] Now, that would be world changing.

Confront our mortality

Along with everyone who has ever walked on the planet, the one guaranteed thing about life is that as soon as we are born, we will at some point die. Living fully and dying consciously is about looking at things from this higher perspective. When we consciously accept our mortality, we see life differently. We know it's finite. An end will come. This makes us truly value what we have, and to do the best we possibly can while we still have life left in our body. Therefore, if your life isn't working for you, do something about it!

I recognise that facing death is an entirely different matter from facing extinction. This takes the concept of mortality to a completely new level. But, when we connect with the bigger picture of who we are, we see ourselves for what we truly are – a blink in the eye of the Universe. Look what happened when the dinosaurs and most of life on Earth were wiped out. It took a while, but the planet replenished, life recalibrated and human beings, alongside countless other species, thrived. In whatever way the planet transmutes, life *will* continue – it's impossible to destroy life because life is consciousness. It's just that it may not continue in the form of life we experience at the moment, and certainly not in the vast numbers we have currently reached, which is no bad thing. If you really want a reality check on our importance as a species spend some time reflecting on the extraordinary and beautiful photograph taken by Voyager 1 as it passed out of our solar system on February 14th, 1990, 3.7 billion miles from Earth.[77] Our planet is a minute, pale, blue dot, almost invisible in the vast expanse of space.

Form groups

My counsel to anyone struggling to make sense of the changes that are knocking at the door is to form or join a group of people whom you meet with regularly; people who are willing to be honest and open about what's going on in the world, yet are not prepared to indulge in doom saying (this really doesn't help) or have the unrealistic expectation that everything will suddenly be fine. It's about accepting the reality of what's going on and agreeing to focus on what is inspiring for you all.

Joanna Macy and Chris Johnstone write about how much we now need to form groups in their book, *Active Hope: How to Face the Mess we're in without going crazy.* Coming together in a group provides a foundation of courage and resilience so we can adapt as circumstances change, see setbacks for what they are, and find strength when times look bleak. They say, 'When conditions are difficult, having a trusted gang around us both to draw from, and give to, can make all the difference.' I have experienced the same resilience when running Death Cafés. We *need* to come together to connect and care for each other when we engage with uncomfortable situations.

Stand up and say NO!

Although much harm and destruction have been done without our consent or even knowledge, every one of us is complicit in the way we human beings have wreaked havoc across the planet. Ignorance is not an excuse. We are clearly desecrating our beautiful Mother Earth and we have to find ways to stop it. This is not about feeding the fear of possible extinction. It's about using fear to trigger action that changes how things currently stand.

I salute Rebellion Extinction, 350 and similar environmental and sustainability organisations for their ceaseless and often vilified work on insisting that governments across the world take urgent climate crisis action. And, I am in awe of sixteen-year-old Swedish environmentalist, Greta Thunberg, who, together with a host of other highly concerned and courageous youngsters, is galvanizing people across the globe to oppose the damage that massive petrochemical and technological corporations and industries are doing to the environment. At this very moment of writing, thousands of Extinction Rebellion activists are gumming up the streets of London in peaceful protest. Others are doing the same in capital cities across the world. If politicians won't listen because they are too embroiled in outmoded personal and political power battles, which distract them from what's really important, people power is forcing them listen. 'The great threat to our planet, says explorer Robert Swan, 'is the belief that someone else will save it.'

More than at any other time in human history, we need to pay homage to our beautiful Mother Earth. We have to remember that what we do to her, we do to ourselves. So, this is the moment to remind ourselves of her amazing gifts, which take us beyond who we believe we are.

'We all can have those transcendent moments during the day when we are caught by the sight of a bird or a flower or a stream of sunlight,' says clinical psychologist John Waite.

It's really easy to feel hopeless about the mess we have got ourselves into. But if there's enough people wanting to shift consciousness away from global capitalism into a new way of being, I believe we can do it. We need to develop compassion for the Earth. This is the only way forward and to take on board that death is pretty laid back really. It doesn't have to go hunting. Everything naturally gravitates towards it so there's no point in fighting it.

I also think it's important to say that nature is not a victim. Yes, what we are doing has severe consequences for lots of species, but we are not going to destroy the Earth. It's an incredible robust system, which will adapt and replenish, with or without us. We think everything exists for us, but it doesn't.

Nature helps us to release ourselves from the traumas and dramas of life. When this happens, we lose our self-consciousness and relax into a place of 'I'm okay, and you're okay, too'. Life becomes easier because we are able to meet with others who are also open to mutual support and encouragement.

Finding our 'tribe' also helps us to feel safe and secure and this supports us to go beyond anxiety, doubt and self-criticism. There's a conscious growth process going on. We may never be completely free of our neurosis, but awareness has a freedom to it. We can observe ourselves falling into the traps of our own making and do something about it.

I see consciousness as a continual process of learning and developing emotional intelligence. It's stepping away from the demands and expectations of 'main stream' consciousness where we are told what to feel and what to think. We stop clinging to particular ways of existing. Instead we become connected to the wonders of what is and develop an amazement for the planet we live on. There's the art that people create and then there's the art that nature creates.

When we continue to live the conventional way, we distance ourselves from nature and alienate ourselves from mortality. We try to sanitise it and regulate it. We believe life is one of competition rather than one of community and connection. But when we begin to realise and accept that we are just passing through – that life is finite – it has a profound effect. Similar to many people who are diagnosed with terminal illness, it makes us want to live more fully and truly appreciate the natural world.

I want to die in the company of my daughter and grandson. I want to have said my goodbyes so it's okay to let go of those in my tribe. I want to be buried in the earth so there's a slow process of disintegration as nature intends and I want the nutrients from my body to seep into the soil to feed the plants and creatures around me. It's being part of nature – there's a sense that my burial will naturally return my body to nature. This gives me great comfort.

This just leaves me to say that it's been a pleasure to travel through this book with you. I hope it's helped you to embrace the importance of living fully and dying consciously. And, when your time comes to go home – however you have experienced your life journey – I hope it reminds you that you will be greeted with a love so exquisite that words cannot describe it.

Human beings are entering an extraordinary, challenging new era, but, one way or another, humanity needs to evolve into a new state of being. We have exhausted the old paradigm. Let's help each other to take off that shabby old jumper filled with holes so future generations can put on another one created out of material that we currently may not know even exists – woven by the Love and Light of the Universe.

When I begin my journey home, I would like to be alone. I would like the space and stillness to be present to every moment of my transition. I want to know what it feels like to step out of my body, back into Love. I want to look back on my life and think, 'Well, gal, you had one hell of ride and you did quite well, considering all.' Then to turn inward to the 'Me' who I have always been and hold out my hands to whatever comes next.

References

Introduction

i   https://www.huffpost.com/entry/a-quantum-theory-of-consciousness_b_596fb782e4b04dcf308d29bb

ii   https://www.facebook.com/livingconsciouslyforabetterworld/?modal=admin_todo_tour

iii   www.deathcafe.com

Section 1

1   https://www.vox.com/explainers/2017/7/19/15925506/psychic-numbing-paul-slovic-apathy

2   https://www.ecology.com/birth-death-rates/

3   https://www.harleystreetaesthetics.com/blog/dr-kremers-blog/2018/05/25/what-is-driving-millennials-to-botox-and-dermal-fillers

4   https://www.chroniclelive.co.uk/news/north-east-news/care-home-nurse-who-failed-12848281

5 http://paloaltoprize.com

6 https://alcor.org/cryomyths.html

7 https://en.wiktionary.org/wiki/
   today_is_a_good_day_to_die

8 https://www.allaboutspirituality.org/reincarnation.htm

9 http://www.buddhanet.net/e-learning/dharmadata/fdd47.
   htm

10 https://www.ancient-origins.net/history/hidden-beliefs-
    covered-church-resurrection-and-reincarnation-early-
    christianity-006320

11 Reed, Jonathan, L. *The Harper Collins Visual Guide to the
    New Testament*

12 Ibid

    https://www.disclose.tv/reincarnation-was-intentionally-
    removed-from-the-bible-evidence-suggests-336295

13 https://www.biola.edu/blogs/good-book-blog/2016/
    why-were-some-books-left-out-of-the-bible

Section 2

14 A. N. Schore, "Effects of a Secure Attachment Relationship
    on Right Brain Development, Affect Regulation and Infant
    Mental Health," Infant Mental Health Journal 22, 1-2 (2001):
    7-66.

15 Foor, Daniel, Ancestral Medicine: rituals for personal and
    family healing

16 https://en.wikipedia.org/wiki/Shuar

17 https://www.justiceforwomen.org.uk/sally-challen-appeal

18 https://www.citizensadvice.org.uk/family/gender-violence/
    domestic-violence-and-abuse-organisations-which-give-
    information-and-advice/

19 https://scholarworks.iu.edu/dspace/handle/2022/23526

20 https://www.psychologytoday.com/us/blog/in-flux/201211/
    you-are-what-you-believe

21 http://trauma-recovery.ca/resiliency/
    post-traumatic-growth/

22 https://www.dailymotion.com/video/x716d04

23 https://thepsychologist.bps.org.uk/volume-27/edition-7/
    emdr-more-just-therapy-ptsd

24 https://heatherplett.com/tag/spiritual-bypassing/

25 https://www.sciencedirect.com/science/article/pii/
    S0262407913623350

26 https://www.jodivine.com/articles/sexual-health/
    why-the-over-50s-are-not-practising-safe-sex

27 https://myemail.constantcontact.com/Richard-Rohr-s-
    Meditation--Stumbling-and-Falling.html?soid=11030986
    68616&aid=UkPxHNnUqFk

28 www.dwayne-fields.com

29 www.theforgivenessproject.com

Section 3

30 www.atpweb.org/trps-47-15-01-44.pdf

31 https://www.genome.gov/about-genomics/fact-sheets/
    Deoxyribonucleic-Acid-Fact-Shee

32 www.asbmb.org/asbmtoday/201108/features/Goodsell/

33 https://www.forbes.com/sites/quora/2017/12/20/what-is-a-
    quantum-field-and-how-does-it-interact-with-matter/

34 https://futurism.com/what-is-nothing

35 www.scientifivamerican.com/article/
    changing-our-dna-though-mind-contol/

36 www.heartmath.org/articles-of-the-heart/
    personal-development/you-can-change-you

[37] www.lesbrown.com

[38] https://video.search.yahoo.com/search/video?fr=aaplw&p=
YOu+tube+what+is+zero+point+field&guccounter=1#id=
1&vid=4dc0217fabe053e5ea2f91ac4f8edd43&action=view

[39] www.grammarist.com/usage/quantum/

[40] www.rationalwiki.org/wki/Quantum_consciousness

[41] www.youtube.com/watch?v=LGd8p-GSLgY Christof Koch

[42] https://www.youtube.com/watch?v=BQl69hgsFm0.

[43] https://en.wikipedia.org/wiki/Holon_(philosophy)

[44] https://chopra.com/articles/
how-to-recognize-signs-from-the-universe

[45] www.decision-making-solutions.com/intuitive_
decisions_making.html

[46] Childre, Doc, et al *Heart Intelligence: connecting with the
intuitive guidance of the heart*

[47] https://www.consciouslifestylemag.com/
heart-intelligence/

[48] https://www.youtube.com/watch?v=mvf5kNbukG0

[49] https://upliftconnect.
com/12-ways-unlock-powers-vagus-nerve/

[50] http://www.mbraining.com/mbit-and-leadership

[51] www.guardian.com/lifeandstyle/2016/feb/03/
death-doulas-women-who-stay-by-your-side-to-the-end

[52] https://www.amazon.co.uk/Nearing-End-Life-Relatives-
Friends-ebook/dp/B00CKOXCPY/ref=sr_1_1?keywords
=nearing+the+end+of+life&qid=1573126357&sr=8-1

[53] End-of-life Experiences: Reaching out for compassion,
communication and connection. Meaning of Deathbed
Visions and Coincidences. American Journal of Palliative
Care, Volume 28 (1): 7 Feb 1, 2011

[54] End of Life Experiences: Reaching out for Compassion,,
Communication and Connection: meaning of deathbed

visions and coincidence. American Journal of Palliative Care, Vol 28 (1) Feb 1, 2011, Fenwick, P & Brayne S.

55   www.newscientist.com/article/mg22329762-700-consciousness-on-off-switch-discovered-deep-in-the-brain

56   https://www.psychologytoday.com/gb/blog/sleepless-in-america/201010/the-mysterious-benefits-deep-sleep

https://www.sciencealert.com/brain-activity-recorded-as-much-as-10-minutes-after-death-human-science

57   https://www.psychologytoday.com/gb/blog/sleepless-in-america/201010/the-mysterious-benefits-deep-sleep

58   https://www.youtube.com/watch?v=78SkTuk8Zd4

59   https://www.wired.com/2013/08/after-death-consciousness-rats/

60   https://www.sciencedaily.com/releases/2014/10/141007092108.htm

61   https://www.telegraph.co.uk/science/2016/03/12/first-hint-of-life-after-death-in-biggest-ever-scientific-study/

62   https://www.youtube.com/watch?v=yByEQfaD314

63   https://www.youtube.com/watch?v=lK3xsZpU3zw

64   https://www.youtube.com/watch?v=DAZJtFZZYmM

Final Chapter

65   https://en.wikipedia.org/wiki/End_time

66   https://www.crystalinks.com/hopi2.html

67   https://www.youtube.com/watch?v=6ucn3Xswv4Q

68   Arguelles, Jose *The Mayan Factor: the path beyond technology*,

69   https://grahamhancock.com/dmisrab6/

[70] https://www.3ho.org/3ho-lifestyle/aquarian-age/aquarian-shift-what-will-be-different

[71] https://www.abc.net.au/news/science/2019-01-25/earths-magnetic-poles-are-moving-but-dont-flip-out/10727276

[72] https://www.sciencetimes.com/articles/5453/20150406/global-climate-change-the-earth-has-shifted-say-inuit-elders.htm

[73] https://www.nationalgeographic.com/science/2019/02/magnetic-north-update-navigation-maps/

[74] https://www.youtube.com/watch?v=d0fm7YlX8AY

[75] https://edition.cnn.com/2019/05/07/health/climate-anxiety-eprise/index.html

[76] https://en.wikipedia.org/wiki/Seven_generation_sustainability

[77] http://www.astronomytrek.com/10-interesting-facts-about-the-voyager-1-probe/

Suggested Reading

~

A Book of Silence: a journey in search of the pleasures and powers of silence, Sara Maitland

A New Earth: create a better life, Eckhart Tolle

A Return to Love, Marianne Williamson

Active Hope: how to face the mess we're in within without going crazy, Joanna Macey & Chris Johnstone

An Introduction to Religious & Spiritual Experiences, Marianne Rankin

Anam Cara: spiritual wisdom from the Celtic world, John O'Donoghue

Chicken Soup for the Soul, Jack Canfield

Consciousness beyond life: the science of near-death experiences, Pim van Lommel

Destiny of Souls: new cases of life between life, Michael Newton

Dreams at the Threshold, Jeanne Van Bronkhorst

Energy Blessings from the Stars, Virginia Essene & Irving Feurst

Falling Upwards, Richard Rohr

279

The Divine Matrix, Gregg Braden

Healing into Life & Death, Stephen Levine

Heart Intelligence: connecting with the intuitive guidance of the heart, Doc Childre et al

Hope and Grace: Spiritual Experiences in Severe Distress, Illness and Dying, Monica Renz

I am I, Saraswami Ma

Is There Life After Death?: the extraordinary science of what happens when we die, Anthony Peake

Know Yourself, Ernest Holmes

Living Mystery: what lies between Science and Religion, Mark Hederman

Man's Search for Meaning, Viktor Frankl

My Journey through time: a spiritual memoir of life, death, and rebirth. Dena Merriam

My Stroke of Genius, Jill Bolte Taylor

On Death and Dying, Elisabeth Kubler-Ross

One, Richard Bach

Out of the Darkness: from turmoil to transformation, Steve Taylor

Ponder On This: A Compilation, Alice Bailey

Proof of Heaven: a neurosurgeon's journey into the afterlife, Dr Eben Alexander

Resilience from the Heart: the power to thrive in life's extremes, Gregg Braden

Sex, Meaning, and the Menopause, Sue Brayne

Silence: the power of quiet in a world full of noise, Thich Nhat Hanh

Start From Where You Are: how to accept yourself and others, Pema Chodron

Testimony of Light: an extraordinary message of life after death, Helen Greaves

The Ancestral Continuum: unlock the secrets of who you really are, Natalia O'Sullivan and Nicola Graydon

The Art of Dying, Peter and Elizabeth Fenwick

The Biology of Belief, Bruce Lipton

The D-Word: talking about dying, Sue Brayne

The Divine Arsonist – A Tale of Awakening, Jacob Nordby

The Divine Matrix, Gregg Braden

The Field, Lynne McTaggart

The Good Gut, Justin Sonnenburg & Erica Sonnenburg

The Science of Being (1923), Baron Eugene Ferson

The Untethered Soul: the journey beyond yourself, Michael A. Singer

The Wisdom of Near-Death Experiences, Penny Satori

Towards a Meaningful Life, Menachem Mendel Scheerson

Using Your Multiple Brains to do Cool Stuff, Grant Soosalu and Marvin Oka

Waking the Tiger: healing trauma, Peter A Levine

You Can Change Your Life: a future different from your past with Hoffman Process, Tim Laurence

Index

Lightning Source UK Ltd.
Milton Keynes UK
UKHW010637260722
406393UK00002B/569